Burnout:
The New Academic Disease

by Winifred Albizu Meléndez and Rafael M. de Guzmán

ASHE-ERIC/Higher Education Research Report No. 9, 1983

Prepared by

 Clearinghouse on Higher Education
The George Washington University

Published by

Association for the Study of Higher Education

Jonathan D. Fife,
Series Editor

Cite as:
Meléndez, Winifred Albizu and de Guzmán, Rafael M. *Burnout: The New Academic Disease*. ASHE-ERIC Higher Education Research Report No. 9. Washington, D.C.: Association for the Study of Higher Education, 1983.

The ERIC Clearinghouse on Higher Education invites individuals to submit proposals for writing monographs for the Higher Education Research Report series. Proposals must include:
1. A detailed manuscript proposal of not more than five pages.
2. A 75-word summary to be used by several review committees for the initial screening and rating of each proposal.
3. A vita.
4. A writing sample.

ISSN 0737-1292
ISBN 0-913317-08-X

ERIC Clearinghouse on Higher Education
The George Washington UIniversity
One Dupont Circle, Suite 630
Washington, D.C. 20036

Association for the Study of Higher Education
One Dupont Circle, Suite 630
Washington, D.C. 20036

This publication was partially prepared with funding from the National Institute of Education. U.S. Department of Education, under contract no. 400-82-0011. The opinions expressed in this report do not necessarily reflect the positions or policies of NIE or the Department.

Richard Lonsdale
Professor of Educational Administration
New York University

Linda Kock Lorimer
Associate General Counsel
Yale University

Virginia B. Nordby
Director
Affirmative Action Programs
University of Michigan

Eugene Oliver
Director, University Office of School & College Relations
University of Illinois—Champaign

Harold Orlans
Lawyer

Marianne Phelps
Assistant Provost for Affirmative Action
The George Washington University

Gary K. Probst
Professor of Reading
Prince Georges Community College

Cliff Sjogren
Director of Admissions
University of Michigan

Al Smith
Assistant Director of the Institute of Higher Education &
    Professor of Instructional Leadership & Support
University of Florida

CONTENTS

FOREWORD

For the most part, higher education institutions have not faced any single cataclysmic event that has threatened their very survival. Some institutions have had to close their doors and others have merged, but on the whole, at least outwardly, colleges and universities appear to be not very different than they were in the 1960s. Events that have affected them have been subtle and gradual. However, even gradual erosion can eventually damage a foundation. Our institutions may find that they no longer can successfully fulfill their missions.

Many of the events affecting academe, such as enrollment declines and financial pressures, have been addressed in previous Research Reports. This Report focuses on the psychological and physiological results of these events. The following scene is becoming increasingly common-place at many institutions:

A highly talented and enthusaistic individual is hired to perform a particular job. Having demonstrated success at that job, other tasks and responsibilities are assigned or accepted. As financial conditions worsen, responsibilities continue to expand while support staff and services shrink. Frustration builds as the individual is no longer able to achieve the level of excellence once considered normal. Finally, exhausted from working long hours, new patterns of behavior emerge in order to face a job that is no longer enjoyable. Eventually, the individual either quits or develops a coping mentality and work pattern that makes survival possible until retirement. In short, the individual's enthusiasm and commitment have burned out.

This issue of burnout is one of increasing importance to institutions, because it usually strikes the most competent and committed, the ones who feel strongly about the value of what they are doing and who want to do the best job. Generally, precursors of burnout are easily identifiable: increased demands, conflicting roles and a feeling of loss of control of one's life. In the short run, this may not be detrimental. The long run, something must be done to bring the situation back into control before burnout occurs.

In this Research Report by Winifred Albizu Meléndez, Professor in the College of Humanities at Inter American

University and Rafael M. de Guzmán, Associate Professor of Psychiatry at the University of Puerto Rico Medical School, the literature concerning burnout is thoroughly examined. In the final sections, the authors develop specific ways that institutions can minimize or eliminate the effect of burnout. Attention to this personnel consideration will help a college or university preserve its very foundation: committed and enthusiastic administrative staff and faculty dedicated to the missions of the institution.

Jonathan D. Fife
Director and Series Editor
ERIC Clearinghouse on Higher Education
The George Washington University

ACKNOWLEDGMENTS

Our special acknowledgments must begin with our gratitude to Dr. Jonathan D. Fife, director and series editor, for his indulgence and many considerations. We wish to express special thanks for a grant given by the Research Institute, directed by Dr. Janice Petrovich. Our work was facilitated by the support of Inter American University's Chancellor Rafael Cartagena, Dean Constantino Alvarez, Dean Luis Diaz Soler, and Professor Beatrice Tobin, and by the university librarians, Bruni Perez and Olga Hernandez.

Appreciation is due to Dr. Israel Ramos Perea for his collaboration in the statistical analysis of the study.

A network of colleagues contributed to the accomplishment of this research report. Elba Tirado aided with the research investigation on burnout, Angela Nieves performed many kindnesses buttressing our professional lives, Hortensia Ocasio generously assisted with the statistical analysis, and Lotta Rieskohl counseled, read, and edited the work. If we have not heeded all her warnings, the blame is ours. We are grateful to Miriam Solero Rubio for her efforts in typing and retyping the manuscript.

Finally, we also want to thank Josefina de Guzmán, José A. Meléndez, and Maria and Rafael Albizu, whose presence in our lives enormously eased and sustained all our labors.

EXECUTIVE SUMMARY

Is Burnout a Disease?

Burnout, a faddish and threatening term in today's working place, has been labeled a disease reaching the level of an epidemic.

> *Burnout runs through the teaching profession like Asian flu—possibly because it depresses people to be physically assaulted by those they are trying to civilize. Two years ago, Willard McGuire, president of the National Educational Association, said that burnout among teachers "threatens to reach hurricane force if it isn't checked soon." Social workers and nurses burn out from too much association with hopelessness. Police officers burn out. Professional athletes burn out. Students burn out. Executives burn out. Housewives burn out. And, as every parent knows, there usually comes a moment in late afternoon when baby burnout occurs—all of his little circuits overloaded, the child feels too wrought up to fall asleep* (Marrow 1981, p. 84).

Understanding the concept and learning how to overcome the condition have been the major concerns of industrial-organizational psychologists. More recently, researchers and practitioners have begun to concentrate their attention on burnout in studies that treat the topic externally and symptomatically within the school organization. Only a few have been concerned about the impact it has had on faculty and administrators in academe.

Burnout is a state of mind that afflicts people who work with other people and give much more than what they get in return from their colleagues, friends, supervisors, and clients (Pines, Aronson, and Kafry 1981). The malaise includes such symptoms as lack of enthusiasm for work, helplessness, and frustration. To burn out, people actually need to have felt challenged and excited during the early years of their job.

What is the correlation between work stress, job burnout, and burnout in academe with the vast literature on stress? National surveys show heightened interest about tension and anxiety leading to stress at work (Coates and Thoreson 1976; Freudenberger and North 1982). Increasing pressures on teachers have led to an awareness of the syndrome in education.

To burn out, people actually need to have felt challenged and excited during the early years of their job.

Is stress our friend or our enemy? Can work stress help or hinder our lives? Work stress has already been singled out as a prime determinant of certain positive and/or negative outcomes that may change the psychological, behavioral, and physical well-being of the individual within the work organization. While negative stress can damage physical and emotional health and thus ruin a career (Levinson 1970; McGaffey 1978; Student 1978), positive stress on the other hand can stimulate motivation and bring forth challenge to the job (Meglino 1977; Sales 1969a; Selye 1974). In fact, some stress may even be advantageous in decision making as a function of eustress (Janis 1958, 1972).

How serious is the problem of burnout in academe? The concept of burnout is a well-known phenomenon as it applies to the helping professions. Maslach and Freudenberger conducted pioneering research in the helping professions and brought the findings to nationwide attention. In academe, however, it is still an enigma. The syndrome has increased in seriousness because of its physical and emotional affliction upon teachers at elementary and high school levels. A plethora of research indicates that burnout is a significant problem facing contemporary education.

The literature on professional autonomy indicates that faculty relate best to each other as equals on an informal level. Communal efforts and support are important aspects of professionalism, for included in the profile of a professional is the desire for collegiality (Pankin 1973). Faculty instead labor in a bureaucracy imposing organizational restrictions and obstructed relationships. This incompatibility between professional autonomy and bureaucratic formalization elicits conflicting strategies that impede instructors' productivity (Clagett 1980; McGee 1971). Simply put, the freshness of spontaneity and creativity has flown.

Why Do Some Burn Out and Others Cope?
The tragedy of burnout is that the malaise impacts precisely on idealistic, enthusiastic, and energetic persons. An individual who is indifferent to his job will be least likely to burn out. "One of the great costs of burnout is the diminution of the effective service of the very best people in a given profession" (Pines, Aronson, and Kafry 1981, p. 4).

A conceptual model of work stress also helps to answer the question. The Person-Environment Fit Model constructs a framework for much of the current research and thought in the field of occupational stress (MacBride 1982). The theoretical model includes both the personal and organizational factors linked to job stress and to negative health outcomes. This approach adopts the widest possible range of phenomena. Thus, burnout fits under its conceptual roof.

The P-E fit model specifically focuses on the affinity between the subject's personality, needs, and abilities and the environment's capacity to make appropriate use of them. For instance, any high-, moderate-, and low-stress job can lead to burnout. The key factor is learning how to manage it, and above all learning how to identify which stage of burnout prevails at the particular moment (Veninga and Spradley 1981).

More recently stress has been viewed as the product of a misfit between the individual and his environment. This idea, formulated in the P-E fit model, holds that the combination of an individual, including his particular personality and behaviors, with a particular physical and social environment can result in a stressful situation or imbalance. Stressors from both domains beseige the individual.

Can Burnout Be Prevented?
Strategies for preventing or treating burnout can be viewed from two perspectives: the personal and the organizational. Personal strategies include the management of stressful feelings and situations by following Hans Selye's philosophy of "altruistic egoism" and by using his prescription for enjoying a full life.

Organizational strategies refer to the implementation of new reward systems, adult-career development programs, informal communication styles, and the involvement of faculty in planning and in governance of institutions. By supporting faculty and promoting institutional vitality, decision makers can foster creativity and productivity among faculty. This is the best medicine in the academic market for preventing or treating initial symptoms of burnout.

Can Academia Survive Burnout?
It has become apparent that retrenchment continues to be a way of life in academe. The situation is cause for alarm

because faculty careers have been affected the most. Along with this trend, many individuals appear to have lost their identity with academe. Pressures originally leading to faculty stress will persist in the future; hence, institutions at this point need to become more aware of the effects of stress upon their faculty and administrators.

All available resources and personnel should join forces to quell the effects of this incipient and rampant disease, destined to harm the very people whose goal it is to serve others with greater understanding and insight. In academia, scholars abound who are willing and able to contribute to knowledge on stress and, like dedicated doctors treating their patients (in this case themselves), finding effective ways to penetrate the mystery of an ailment threatening their very life's work.

Academia has infinite opportunity for survival if it can stop the burnout epidemic immediately.

MEANINGS: From Burnout to Stress to Burnout in Academe

Burnout

It is not exciting anymore to wake up in the morning, dress, and go to work. It has been some time since you had any enthusiasm for your job. It is not challenging anymore and has simply become a drag. You are constantly tired, suffer continuous headaches, and cannot get rid of a cold. You could be suffering from "burnout."

Stress resides in all individuals, but burnout is a distinctive kind of work-related stress. Among corporate managers, the word is becoming socially acceptable (Greenberger 1981). It is a slick way of expressing one's tiredness, frustrations, and cynicism regarding work. An estimated 10 percent of the overall executive population show symptoms of job burnout (Manuso 1979): "exhaustion, detachment, boredom and cynicism, impatience and heightened irritability, a sense of impotence, a feeling of being unappreciated, paranoia, disorientation, psychosomatic complaints, depression, and denial of feelings" (Freudenberger 1980, p. 61).

The phenomenon of burnout originally focused on the "helping professions" or "human services" (Cherniss 1980), such as social work. Studies on the subject have extended to other helping professions, such as nursing and teaching, and more recently to other occupations that generate considerable stress, such as business and corporate work, in which the syndrome has been quite evident. It is the continuous interpersonal relationship between professional and client that causes emotional exhaustion, creates stress, and finally changes an individual's behavior. Maslach, who conducted the pioneering research, defines burnout as "a syndrome of emotional exhaustion and cynicism that frequently occurs among individuals who do 'people work'—spend considerable time in close encounters with others under conditions of chronic tension and stress" (Maslach and Jackson 1979). Burnout is thus specifically viewed as a phenomenon related to job stress (Maslach 1982b).

It should be evident by now that burnout is not just a malaise or indisposition; rather, it has advanced into an unwholesome state or condition that can bring highly unpleasant feelings and reactions, including overt and covert "dis-ease," and can threaten one's job status. As in the case of any situation with strong impact and the connota-

[B]urnout is a distinctive kind of work-related stress.

tion of adverse or harmful consequences, burnout also sets into motion a protective response that nature has provided for the purpose of survival. This protective response is called "the stress reaction." Because its implications for health and disease are vast, it merits a careful review.

Stress
Government leaders, scientists, and the general public have joined in their increasing concern to try to understand stress in its relationship to the medical, social, behavioral, and organizational sciences. Insights on stress that are relevant to burnout provide a broader view and understanding of that subject.

According to the original scientific definition:

> *Stress is the state manifested by a specific syndrome which consists of all the nonspecifically induced changes within a biological system* (Selye 1965, p. 54).

Stress is "both specific and nonspecific at the same time" (Selye 1983a, p. 5). Effort, fatigue, pain, and fear produce stress, but none can be singled out as the one factor, because stress applies equally to all (Selye 1974, p. 12). Certain features are common to all of them. Stress can be the outside cause of one's reaction and also the reaction itself. Medically, however, the term is applied only to the reaction (Oken 1974).

The price of stress is high, for it simultaneously affects society's emotional and physical health on many levels. Ambivalence about family, alienation of children, conflicting roles for men and women, an impersonal working environment, and a highly technological society are just a few of the current conditions influencing stress. Not everyone, however, interprets these same events as threatening or stressful (Groen and Bastiaans 1975; Kneller 1965; Ryan 1969); what may be stressful to one person may not necessarily affect another (Oken 1974, p. 10).

Physical Stress: Fight or Flight
Selye noted that during its response to stress, the body changes in many ways to mobilize its defenses and guard itself against damage—the "general adaptation syndrome." The changes consist of three stages—the alarm reaction,

resistance, and exhaustion. In the first stage, the brain contacts the pituitary gland, which sends a hormonal message to the adrenal glands, which produce hormones that activate a physiologic response (Selye 1974). The physiological phenomenon begins from the moment the adrenal glands enlarge as the lymphatic glands shrink. One breathes heavily, thereby increasing heart rate and blood pressure and releasing into the bloodstream more cholesterol and chemicals that coagulate the blood. As one feels the need for more oxygen, adrenalin dilates the bronchi to allow a greater intake of oxygen. Hands and feet become cold while perspiration increases because blood flows from the extremities to vital organs. Pupils dilate for maximum vision and digestive processes slow down to send blood to the muscles (Schwartz 1982, p. 13). The body thus prepares itself for fight or flight.

In the second stage, resistance, the body's defenses are mobilized and damage is thereby thwarted. Ideally, during this stage, the individual restores equilibrium. Should the stressors continue unabated and the natural defense mechanisms fail to work, however, the third stage occurs. During exhaustion, adaptive mechanisms collapse and the body encounters the effects of stress-related illness or even death (Selye 1974). Reactions to stress, generated anywhere along the spectrum from simple temperature changes to life-and-death situations, can stimulate one to fight or flee.

Psychological Aspects of Stress
The environmental stimulus and the reacting individual are both crucial in the response to stress.

Psychological stress resides neither in the situation nor in the person; it depends on a transaction between the two. It arises from how the person appraises an event and adapts to it. Stress is what occurs when the demands of the environment, in the person's eyes, clearly exceed the resources of the person to handle them. Foremost among those resources is how the person construes the situation: does he or she judge it as threatening, or as a challenge? (Richard S. Lazarus quoted in Goleman 1979, p. 52).

Thus, for Lazarus, "the intervening processes—the thoughts we have about an impending threat, the actions we take to avoid it"—are most important (Goleman 1979, p. 44).

Many events in an individual's life are depressing; others make one feel embarrassed or angry. The same situation evokes different reactions in various individuals. Each feeling has its own physical features; for example, one may perspire with the feeling of anxiety but blush because of embarrassment or anger. Psychological stress results from daily pressures and an individual's sensitivities. Vulnerability to stress is frequently related to an individual's inability to adjust to hazardous situations.

A more pressing task confronting researchers is how to identify stressors in routine events. The Holmes-Rahe scale was the first attempt to study both positive and negative events in the lives of thousands of patients who had previous health problems. (The premise for the research was that a succession of major events could become a risk factor for illness.) The data were collected over two decades, and the events were categorized and ranked in terms of intensity.

Lazarus, however, objects to studying stress in terms of accumulated events. Small daily stresses, or hassles, are just as important as the milestone stresses that the Holmes-Rahe scale measures. In referring to the Hassle Scale, Lazarus notes that "the constant, minor irritants may be much more important than the large, landmark changes." He explains further:

A person's morale, social functioning, and health don't hinge on hassles alone, but on a balance between the good things that happen to people—that make them feel good—and the bad. . . . There's something else. Remember, how you construe an event determines if it's stressful or not. It's a function of how the person appraises it. Some people, for example, [list] divorce as an uplift (Goleman 1979, p. 52).

Lazarus hopes not only to specify characteristics of hassles but also to establish "hassle norms" for the general population and for particular locales and age groups, such as the New Yorker, the middle-aged businessman, the typical adolescent girl. Such findings about life events could emphasize the complexity of stress and weaken explanations of cause and effect. Longitudinal analyses of people's emotional appraisal patterns and simultaneous coping could also contribute significantly toward the understanding of stress.

The Paradox: Distress/Eustress
Stress is usually thought of as harmful and as an enemy of health. It is, however, not only a normal response but also essential for living. As Selye explains, death will occur in the absence of stress, for without it we could never survive. How would a person operate without the challenges that induce stress?

Selye distinguishes between distress and eustress. While distress and stress are often used interchangeably, individuals must realize that stress takes two forms—one of which is *distress,* the other of which is *eustress* (Selye 1980, p. 11). Both depend not on the event but on an individual's perception of events, and the same event can cause both reactions in different individuals. For instance, the end of World War II caused eustress among Americans because they were the victors, but it meant distress for the Japanese because they were the vanquished. While both come from an individual's collective environment, distress *engages* a series of nonspecific responses within the individual, and eustress *elicits* a specific reaction from the body. For example, a ballet dancer can face eustress by exercising her body three or four hours a day because the body has adapted itself to exercising and has developed a specific mechanical response pattern for exercising through habituation. If a sedentary individual tried to exercise three or four hours a day, however, her body would become highly distressed because it was not acclimated to such rigorous exercising (Frew 1977, p. 90).

A person's life is a chain of interactions between the individual and his environment. Many situations can be considered stressful. Some are good, others bad. Some are *threats,* others *challenges.* Some are *distress,* others *eustress.* Lazarus, for example, conceives of the term stress as the "cognitive appraisal" of an event. A person reacts to the demands of a certain stressor in view of his personal resources for adapting. Should the demands he perceives exceed his available resources, the individual will most probably consider the stressor as a threat; however, should his resources exceed the demands, then the individual will probably consider the stressor as a positive challenge.

Lazarus's *threats* and *challenges* are therefore equivalent to Selye's *distress* (unpleasant and depressing situations) and *eustress* (pleasant and satisfying situations). Evidence indicates that some stress in challenges has enhanced learning (Delgado, Roberts, and Miller 1954; Glazer and Weiss 1976; Miller 1951, 1980) and improved work performance (Anderson 1976; Flowers and Hughes 1973; Frew 1977; Ivancevich and Matteson 1980; Rogers 1983).

Although some individuals can excel in a very stressful situation, research increasingly indicates that excessive stress can result in poor health and/or chronic illness. Stress may be the cause of several disorders—peptic ulcers, high blood pressure, rheumatoid arthritis, thyroid disease, and others. These diseases usually occur during stressful events; Selye calls them the "stress diseases" or "diseases of adaptation." They are also known as "psychosomatic diseases." Emotional reactions play a major role in causing these psychological and physical problems, which then affect either the weakest part or most vulnerable organ of the body.

An individual can protect himself in many ways from the harmful effects of stress. By learning to master the pressures of everyday living, one discovers that stress can become a friend instead of an enemy by converting distress into eustress.

The Connection: Work Stress/Job Burnout
It would be impossible to work efficiently without generating some degree of stress. Adrenalin must flow if one is to do a beneficial job. Stress therefore should not be eliminated from the body's system.

But the cost of stress is high. Stress disorders cost organizations approximately $17 to $25 billion each year in lost performance, absenteeism, and health benefit payments (McGaffey 1978). In 1981, the Washington Business Group on Health, a representative for approximately 500 national corporations, reported that industry is losing more than $1 billion yearly on problems related to stress, resulting in low productivity, loss of time, accidents, and medical costs. An additional $42 billion a year can be attributed to alcohol and drug abuse and dependency, which often occur as reactions to stress.

It is obvious that the impact of stress at work on all phases of living cannot be ignored any longer. Excessive stress is harmful and affects one's health, productivity, and family relationships.

Environmental stressors are categorized as physical or psychosocial. Poor ventilation and lighting and excessive noise fall under the category of physical stressors. Some psychosocial stressors include lack of job satisfaction or work security, little or no recognition for performance. Any one or a combination of these stressors during a prolonged period of time can overload an individual's capacity for stress and trigger physiological responses, thus leading to the stage of exhaustion and to the susceptibility to mental or physical illness, and opening the gateway to burnout.

Executive burnout has many causes. Rapidly changing technology and the problems of retrenchment can create an ambiguous situation, especially for the young executive who enters a profession with much vitality and enthusiasm and plans to advance rapidly in the company. The middle-aged executive may feel that this era is becoming "a young man's world" where he will not fit. The executive silently suffers fears, disappointments, and isolation from family, colleagues, and friends (Constandse 1972). He senses that starting over is "a venture that requires both courage and determination" (Mayer 1978).

But an individual can have a low-stress job or no job at all and still burn out. Such is the case when an individual in a routine factory job feels overlooked in his work and experiences little stimulation, no challenge, and few opportunities for growth or when a bored housewife with nothing to do all day feels caged in her secure suburban home while waiting for her tired executive husband to return after a hectic day at the office (Veninga and Spradley 1981).

A stressful job can result in a case of burnout through progressive symptoms.

1. "The Honeymoon" is the beginning stage; high energy, enthusiasm, and job satisfaction start to wear off.

2. "Fuel Shortage" includes the early symptoms of inefficiency at work: dissatisfaction with the job, fatigued, sleepless nights, increased smoking or drinking, or other means of escape.
3. "Chronic Symptoms" involve one's awareness of physical and psychological symptoms—chronic exhaustion, physical illness, anger, and depression.
4. The "Crisis" stage permits symptoms of burnout to reach an acute phase and to obsess the individual with problems.
5. "Hitting the Wall" is the stage of total professional deterioration and dysfunction of physical and psychological health (Veninga and Spradley 1981, pp. 38–70).

While mild stress can be used as a positive force to stimulate performance and to achieve a rewarding life style, unrelieved stress that gets out of hand can create serious damage to one's life.

Burnout in Academe
Staying in the teaching profession is probably the biggest challenge facing teachers today. Year after year, competent teachers abandon their profession. This exodus stems from a variety of reasons, but probably one of the most meaningful and rapidly growing is burnout.

In New York city, two out of every three teachers laid off one year expressed no interest in returning to the classroom.

In 1966, 9% of teachers surveyed said that if they had it to do over again they would not go into education. By 1976, this figure had jumped to 19% and another 17.5% said they might also reconsider their occupational choice.

An NEA stress survey found teachers disillusioned and distraught, as did similar surveys in Massachusetts, Chicago, New York State, Tacoma, and Tampa.

A national survey conducted by Learning Magazine *showed that 93% of the teachers questioned had experienced feelings of burnout* (Collins and Masley 1980, p. 5).

While burnout among teachers is not an entirely new phenomenon, it hit teachers of the seventies with greater frequency.

"It just isn't worth it," said a New York City teacher who asked not to be identified. "The classes are overflowing with kids who demand and deserve full-time attention. Staff morale is low. Then there is the pervasive threat of violence. Teaching is a 24-hour occupation. I don't care how good you are. After seven to 10 years you burn out" (Reed 1979).

Teaching brings many satisfactions, but the job also has its full share of physical, mental, and emotional pressures, which have increased in recent years. College professors too live in a highly competitive world and are subject to many of the same conflicts as high school teachers.

Because of teachers' dissatisfaction with work or institution, the academic climate of the 1980s indicates a highly stressful environment for faculty. They are cognizant of the dichotomy between their personal expectations and the rewards offered to them by their profession. The exodus of faculty from the academy to private business is growing rapidly. Industries lure faculty with attractive salaries and generous fringe benefits. The teaching profession has lost its public esteem and trust. The ideal of becoming a scholar has become an unrealistic achievement, because the marketplace is saturated with Ph.D.s. For many, academe is no longer an attractive, remunerative, or confident way of life.

The usual compensations of tenure and promotion have been diminished, while other, more informal values exert pressures between the individual and the institution. It is becoming almost impossible to achieve security through tenure. Requirements for a promotion include a set number of publications, which takes precedence over the professor's effective and successful teaching. The reward system does not value quality teaching even though most professors regard it as a major responsibility.

Even though the extrinsic rewards of the academy have lost their savor, many professors enter or continue in academe because they pursue intrinsic values: teaching, collegiality, knowledge, respect, and service. "These intrinsic

[T]he academic climate of the 1980s indicates a highly stressful environment for faculty.

values are still the driving force behind faculty careers" (Newell and Spear 1982, p. 5). Although many find professorship a satisfying career, they are sensitive to the incompatibility between their personal professional goals and those of the institution.

Studies reveal that faculty blame many of their dissatisfactions on the internal structure of institutions (McGee 1971) and on having too little involvement in planning and in governance (Magarrell 1982). Policies and practices often negate professors' opinions; thus, academics feel less involved in the important decisions about running an institution. Faculty have individual sets of values and goals to reconcile personal satisfactions, while institutions establish overall rules and regulations whose implications are contrary to accommodating the needs of individuals.

The degree of commitment and purpose in the organization and profession differs among faculty and institutions (Clagett 1980). Instructors' concept of purpose—seeing themselves as part of an association—may be at odds with the institution's purpose—seeing itself as a bureaucracy.

> *Usually included in the definition of professionalism is some notion of collegiality. Professionals are seen relating to each other as a group of equals on an informal and "primary-like" level. The imposition of more formal relationships is often resisted. . . . The organization tends to impose formal relationships on professionals, while professionals prefer [the] collegial relationship. . . . [These] "primary-like" informal relationships are the opposite of those that the organization requires to operate at its most efficient level, i.e., formal relationships. The conflicts between professionals and their organization may be explained, therefore, by recognizing that two different types of social relationships may be operative, i.e., collegiality and formal relationships. When these two types of social relationships operate together, conflict is inevitable (Pankin 1973, pp. 96–97).*

Several areas are sources of possible conflict:

> *First, the professional is bound by a norm of service while a bureaucrat's primary responsibility is to the organization. Second, professional authority is based on*

technical knowledge while bureaucratic authority rests on a legal contract backed by formal sanctions. Third, professional decisions are based on internalized professional standards while bureaucratic decisions represent compliance with directives from superiors. Finally, a professional's decision is judged by peers while a bureaucrat's decision is judged by a superior (Miskel and Gerhardt 1974, p. 85).

Increasing pressures on faculty create an unnecessarily stressful environment, which makes individuals feel "pushed" to resign (Pankin 1973) or simply wonder whether the institution really cares.

The incidence of certain events within an organization indicates professional burnout:

(1) high turnover, (2) low morale, (3) "we-they" polarizations, (4) increased concern with bureaucratic "turf," (5) conflicts over authority, (6) scapegoating of organizational leaders, (7) increased absenteeism, and (8) the replacement of informal communication by rigid, role-defined channels (White 1980, p. 4).

Research on the sources of stress among college faculty, although limited in nature and scope, suggests that work stress is the result of dissatisfactions prompted by academic retrenchment, inflation, unemployment, and shifts in the composition of student bodies. Factors inducing stress most frequently cited in one study include lack of faculty participation in decision making, the increase in underprepared students, students' expectations of high grades, apathetic peers, and low salaries (Clagett 1980). Another study indicates that work-related areas of dissatisfaction cluster around functions of organization and management, including advancement, compensation, and institutional organization and policies (Grahn 1981). Yet another study reports that salary, institutional support, and institutional policies are the three highest ranking sources of stress for all faculty (Bender and Blackwell 1982). It is apparent from these studies that faculty are quite concerned with professional and economic security.

The concept of burnout in academe is still an enigma. How vulnerable are faculty to burnout? Which work-related stressors may lead to burnout, and what are the symptoms of burnout among faculty in institutions of higher education? The signs of faculty burnout are many: "physical and emotional exhaustion—and a feeling of being professionally stuck" (Watkins 1982, p. 1), "lack of significance in [one's] work" and "lack of control over [one's] environment" (Ayala Pines quoted in Watkins 1982, p. 8), "the feeling of being locked into a job routine," (LeRoy Spaniol quoted in Reed 1979), the "diminishment of resources in already modest circumstances and the prospects of more such bad news extending to the horizon of distant possibilities" (*Chronicle of Higher Education*, 2 June 1982, p. 14). In short, *burnout in academe is the result of negatively perceived, work-related events or conditions that produce a level of persistent stress resulting in chronic frustration, tiredness or exhaustion, adverse behavior, and inefficiency and/or dysfunction in one's work.*

While burnout has been confused with being professionally stuck, it should not be assumed that the latter is a stage of burnout or a necessary condition for burnout to occur. Burnout is the result of unrelieved stress so that the individual cannot function in his or her work environment because of the total inability to tolerate stress accompanied by a feeling of exhaustion and fatigue. While the burnt out person is incapable of functioning properly, the stuck person is capable of functioning but lacks stimulation or challenge. The individual may eventually become a victim of burnout, however, because he or she is totally bored and indifferent to his or her career growth.

Stress is a well-known aspect of the modern working world and has become prevalent in the educational community. During the last decade, society has struggled with uncertainties rooted in the country's fragile economy, and the educational community has not been immune to those struggles and uncertainties. Academics, like their counterparts in business, have been compelled to adjust their behavior regarding their families, home environments, workplaces, and social styles. Such transformations help to induce excessive stress. The stress factor then becomes a powerful force in academics' performance of their work. The literature regarding the phenomenon as a serious problem in higher education indicates how widespread and intense the feelings of stress are among faculty and administrators, but it appears that decision makers have little awareness of the problem yet. The educational institution must become aware of, and respond to, the faculty member as a whole person. Environmental conditions may be just as important as the human condition, but they must be integrated if academics are to be held accountable for the educational system.

THE INTERRELATIONSHIP:
Person and Environment

Burnout like job stress is attributable not only to apparent sources of stress but also to the relationship between personal and environmental stressors. The Person-Environment Fit Model, a theory of stress advanced by members of the Institute for Social Research at the University of Michigan, describes the interrelationship of the person and the environment. The model maximizes good fit to minimize work stress and contribute to the individual's total personality growth and self-esteem. It provides the framework for much of the current research on work-related stress (MacBride 1982).

Historical Perspective on the Research
Research within the workplace is a somewhat new phenomenon; behavior in work settings has been a major target of interest only since the Industrial Revolution. Early research, which began with the Industrial Revolution and lasted until the early 1900s, focused attention not on the social factors within the workplace but instead on specific job tasks. Interest in social factors began to gather momentum with the birth of the human relations movement. With his assumption of the "Rabble Hypothesis," Elton Mayo, of the Harvard Graduate School of Business Administration, deplored the authoritarian, task-oriented management practices that lacked avenues for satisfying personal needs and that instead stimulated tension, anxiety, and frustration among workers. Mayo called these feelings of helplessness "anomie." Workers felt unimportant, confused, and unattached to their work environment (Hersey and Blanchard 1972). Concomitantly, between 1920 and 1940, sociologists began to show interest in job stress through the identification and solution of problems at organizational gatherings.

These studies of satisfaction with and stress at work were criticized for their lack of concern with such issues as defining methods or conceptualizing stress at work or for focusing on stressors either within the individual or within the organization rather than the relationship between the two. They did not yield the data needed for important findings about the relationship between the worker and the job.

With the end of World War II, as the country emerged from the deprivation of the depression years and the trauma of the war, work came to mean the vehicle to self-actualization, the means to fulfilling expectations for new values and goals. Concomitantly, with the arrival in the United States of many psychoanalysts who fled the Hitler regime, interest in psychiatry and mental health expanded. It was during that period that the team at the Institute for Social Research emerged with its conceptual model for the interrelationship between individual and environment and its effects on work stress and health.

The P-E Fit Model

The new theory of stress was termed the Person-Environment Fit or Congruence Model (Campbell 1974; Caplan 1972; French and Kahn 1962; French, Rodgers, and Cobb 1974; House 1972; Pinneau 1976; Van Harrison 1976). The theory, based on Lewin's and Murray's descriptions of motivational processes, includes two kinds of fit, or matching (or in their absence, two discrepancies), between the individual and the environment: (1) *the objective P-E fit,* which is the matching between the work environment and the individual, independent of perceptions; and (2) *the subjective P-E fit,* which is the matching between the individual and his own perception (the "subjective person") and the work environment and his perception of it (the "subjective environment"). "Work environment" refers to an individual's task or major responsibility at work in coordination with the social, physical, and organizational aspects of the workplace. How do the objective environment and person relate to the subjective environment and person? Two additional discrepancies describe the degree of compatibility (or fit) between the characteristics of the environment and those of the individual.

How does the objective environment and person relate to the subjective environment and person?

> *The individual's* contact with reality *is defined as the discrepancy between the objective environment and the individual's perception of it. The individual's* accuracy of self-assessment *is defined as the discrepancy between the objective person and the individual's subjective perception of self. . . . Each of the four discrepancies . . . represents an important measure of mental health. Good mental health is represented by no discrepancy or low discrepancy for each of the four comparisons* (Van Harrison 1978, pp. 177–78).

The subjective fit between the person and the job environment may result in good mental health when the continued experience of good fit enhances the person's self-esteem (White 1963), increases growth in personality, and improves physical health (Caplan et al. 1976). Poor fit in the workplace can lead to psychological strains like anxiety and insomnia, physiological strains like high blood pressure, and behavioral symptoms like heavy smoking or consumption of alcohol. Should these job-related stressors persist singly or combined, they can culminate in mental illness (exhaustion, depression, or even burnout) or physical illness (heart disease or ulcer).

P-E fit is not a static model of work stress. Stressors can be changed both in the environment and in the person through *coping* or *defense*. Coping refers to altering the objective environment—by changing jobs or requesting a raise, for example—or changing the objective person—by upgrading skills through additional training, for example. In a poor fit, a person employs defense mechanisms to alter the subjective fit (the subjective environment or subjective person) through unconscious mental processes, such as repression or projection (MacBride 1982).

What is the basis for the relationship between the job, the individual, and stress? An individual usually strives to attain a set of goals that he or she has learned to value. The individual's self-concept is enhanced if the goals are met, his well-being impaired if they are not. These concepts are implicit in the fit between the individual and the environment. Stress increases when the environment threatens not to support the goals the individual seeks. The P-E fit model conceptualizes these relationships between forces acting on the individual, identifying the needs and motives separately, and distinguishes between the demands of the work environment and what the work environment offers or supplies. A unique bond must be realized between the individual's needs and values and the work environment. This bond or relationship exists throughout a job period or is considered when one is choosing a career (Van Harrison 1978).

P-E Fit in Academe

What are the implications of the P-E fit theory for faculty in higher education? First, the fit between the faculty candidate and the position available should be contemplated carefully. Several questions need to be answered: What are the candidate's motives or expectations with regard to the position available? What are the purposes of the institution? Is it a liberal arts, technical, or community college, or a university? Is it oriented toward teaching or research? How do the individual and his qualifications fit into the institution's image in the community? What are the opportunities for personal and professional growth?

Once the faculty candidate has been hired, the fit can be periodically reviewed as part of an annual evaluation. It is a fact that people's values, needs, and abilities are continuously changing. With technology playing such an important role in the development and growth of postsecondary institutions, shifts in offers and demands for different positions within institutions occur. For individuals whose environment does not fit, attempts can be made to reduce stress through counseling or additional training. But if the misfit demonstrates the need for more challenging work, then a promotion or its equivalent remuneration should be considered. Fit regarding the faculty's needs and values must be considered in addition to fit regarding individual abilities.

The institution should develop some kind of process for evaluations throughout the professional life of tenured faculty. Developing such a program would not only correct misfits but also maintain productive fits. The usual approach has been for administrator, dean, or chair to continually monitor the fit between faculty member and institution (or department). It is worth considering, however, placing most of the responsibility for reducing stress on the faculty member. If institutions could allow faculty to have greater control over their own obligations and work environment, perhaps then they could themselves modify their individual preferences to effect a better fit with their environment.

Giving the faculty member more control should not be confused with requiring more work. Enriching or enlarging responsibilities may improve fit for some, but it could worsen fit for others who prefer simpler academic lives. Providing more control will, however, make it necessary to meet the challenge of greater faculty involvement. The P-E fit theory suggests that increasing participation incrementally is valid, because it allows the faculty member to structure responsibilities to better fit his abilities and values. For that 20 percent of the faculty with great stamina, who want more complex and challenging tasks, new academic opportunities can be instigated while motivation remains high. The faculty preferring simpler assignments, and in particular those who do not wish to participate in decision making, could relegate that task to others.

The tremendous advantage of allowing some individualization of the job is the creation of a mechanism for the ongoing maintenance of good fit. As either personal preferences or job demands change, the individual can— without outside intervention—cope by making adjustments in the job to lessen [misfit] and improve fit (Van Harrison 1978, p. 198).

Obtaining and maintaining good fit between the individual and his work throughout the entire working career suggests that planning is necessary to maximize good fit throughout all stages of life. Distinctions have to be made between fits at different times. For instance, the effects of a misfit at a current position may be tolerated if the current position is used to reach a future goal. Failed expectations and fits, because of a change in individual needs, values, or abilities or because of a wrong perception of the demands and supplies of one's job, could be remedied by changing the career. More evidence is needed on the use of P-E fit to clarify the selection of career paths and adult life cycles influencing changes in the values and goals of the individual throughout stages in his career.

Other Models of Value
Although the P-E fit theory is one of the most widely accepted models of occupational stress, other concepts are worthy of attention, such as the study based on cybernetics. The basic premise of this theory is that behavior is directed at reducing deviations from a specific goal or state of being (Cummings and Cooper 1979).

A model of teacher stress presented by Kyriacou and Sutcliffe (1979) emphasizes the assessment of threat to one's well-being as a central mechanism mediating the experience of stress. Individuals who in general expect external control are more likely to appraise their environment as threatening and hence may experience greater stress.

According to a model proposed by House and Wells (1978), the three dimensions of the burnout syndrome reflect the three major symptomatic categories of stress: physiological energy; affective-cognitive behavior, which focuses on demoralization and frustration; and behavioral symptoms, which focus on reduced work efficiency. This model reveals social and psychological variables as proposed by Beehr and Newman (1978) and Matteson and Ivancevich (1979).

STRESSORS: Effects within the Person and the Environment

Sigmund Freud said that a mentally healthy individual is someone who is capable of love and work. He pointed out that work allows the individual to stay in touch with his world and at the same time control it. Therefore, he considered work a crucial medium for mental health (Levinson 1970).

> In the mentally healthy person [the id, the ego, and the superego] form a unified and harmonious organization. By working together cooperatively they enable the individual to carry on efficient and satisfying transactions with his environment (Hall 1954, p. 22).

Perish the thought that one could possibly become mentally ill today. Instead, the talk is of stress. Everyone agrees that they experience tremendous pressures from their outside world, business concerns, family life, and a whole round of daily events. Stress, however, is not just something that is aroused by outside sources, such as the workplace, for much has to do with an individual's inner make-up.

The P-E fit model emphasizes the interrelationship between the individual and the work environment. It does not, however, reject the possible effects of stressors within the person or the workplace. The model does not disregard the assumption that because "burnout is caused by prolonged exposure to stress and frustration, all of the various personal and environmental factors that generate stress and frustration for humans must be considered as potential causes of burnout" (Carroll and White 1982).

Factors within the Person

No known personality trait can cause burnout in an individual. Research has shown, however, that certain personality characteristics may predispose an individual to burnout. From clinical experience, Freudenberger (1982) describes two groups of individuals who are prone to burnout. The individuals in one group descend from families whose fathers are authoritative, cold, unaffectionate, socially passive, but occasionally argumentative. The mothers are also cold and authoritative but active as social climbers. Often the individuals of this group refer to themselves as low achievers, very sensitive, and with a desire to be accepted.

The other group seems to have driven, ambitious, achievement-oriented fathers as role models. The mothers in this group are gentle, passive, nurturing persons but not always capable of demonstrating their feelings. The individuals in this group describe themselves as high achievers, sociable, and responsive. In both groups, individuals depict themselves as loners, unable to express feelings or be assertive. Usually they are the very people who invest so much time in their jobs in search of fulfillment and identity. They work with a high sense of idealism and hope. A very important factor is that they are accepted and liked. They give to the point of becoming drained and thus become selfless. But all along they refuse to rely on others or to request help.

Some research relates personality and behavioral traits to stress and ultimately to coronary heart disease. "The most consistent evidence relating psychological factors to [coronary heart disease] appears to be associated with certain personality and behavioral traits" (Rosenman and Friedman 1983, p. 49), such as the Type A behavior pattern, a complex of emotional reactions. In contrast to its "B" counterpart, in which easy-going personality traits predominate, Type A behavior is considered the principal risk factor for coronary heart disease. Type A behavior is

[C]ertain personality characteristics may predispose an individual to burnout.

> *an action-emotion complex that can be observed in any person who is aggressively involved in a chronic, incessant struggle to achieve more and more in less and less time, and if required to do so, against the opposing efforts of other things or other persons. It is not psychosis or a complex of worries or fear or phobias or obsessions, but a socially acceptable—indeed often praised—form of conflict. Persons possessing this pattern also are quite prone to exhibit a free-floating but extraordinarily well-rationalized hostility. As might be expected, there are degrees in the intensity of this behavior pattern. Moreover, because the pattern represents the reaction that takes place when particular personality traits of an afflicted individual are challenged or aroused by a specific environmental agent, the results of this reaction (that is, the behavior pattern itself) may not be felt or exhibited*

by him if he happens to be in or confronted by an environment that presents no challenge (Friedman and Rosenman 1974, pp. 67-68).

Rosenman and Friedman (1983) list 23 psychological and behavioral traits common in Type A behavior, among them self-control, self-confidence, competitiveness, tenseness, impatience, inability to relax away from work, suppressed hostility, an orientation toward achievement, and the denial of failure.

Perhaps the environment of the contemporary university should encourage the increasing prevalence of Type A–style administrators, because such behavior appears to offer special rewards to those who can perform and communicate more aggressively to their colleagues. New partnerships between government/industry and higher education, fomented by spiraling technology, seem to presage the advent of innovative, assertive, and "supersane" administrators.

> *The administrator who knows what real power is and where it comes from will be insulated against burnout. Burnout appears to be a function of the distance between expectations and actuality. The supersane administrator maintains a narrow gap between the two. In the absence of addictions to an idealized image of the way things should be, reality offers few rude surprises. Rewards don't disappear because they issue from within, regardless of fluctuating external circumstance. Neither the system nor the people can make supersane administrators crazy. They accept what is and do what is and do what they do in full recognition that their efforts could fail—[but] at least they had fun getting there. They may choose to leave a job if the enjoyment becomes diminished, but not because they are burnt out. They would have made their move as soon as they sensed it could happen if they stayed longer. Thus, the supersane administrator is in touch with an inner guidance system which will give explicit directions, on time, to anyone who would pay attention* (Vash 1980, p. 114).

Locus of control, self-efficacy, and mastery
Control of a drive or an emotion is a learned process. It includes incessant efforts to find worthwhile, attainable,

aims. When an individual is able to carry forth this process with positive results, he experiences a feeling of self-efficacy and mastery.

We should always strive for what we ourselves—not the society that surrounds us—regard as worthwhile. But we must, at all cost, avoid frustration, the humiliation of failure; we must not aim too high and undertake tasks which are beyond us. Everyone has his own limits. For some of us, these may be near the maximum, for others near the minimum, of what man can attain. But within the limits set by our innate abilities, we should strive for excellence, for the best that we can do. Not for perfection—for that is almost always unattainable—and setting it as an aim can only lead to the distress of frustration. Excellence is a wonderful goal in itself and highly suitable to earn us the goodwill, respect, and even love of our neighbors (Selye 1974, p. 11).

An individual will experience less stress at work and encounter fewer illnesses if he has a strong sense of control over his life (Kyriacou and Sutcliffe 1979). A person who confronts the challenges of a new job experience without proper skills for coping is prone to experience failure on the job, which certainly invites burnout (Warnath 1979).

It is very common these days to find faculty with doctorates teaching at community colleges where they feel trapped in their jobs. They are overqualified and have little opportunity for advancement or even the chance of teaching a course within their specialization. Most damaging is the fact that the individual will probably have to bear with the situation, for the problems of retrenchment at colleges and universities imply the individual has little chance of getting a job at another college. The story could end therefore with the individual's overextending efforts to do the job or with failure and burnout.

The hardy personality type
The notion of control is questioned when one takes into account that some people face stress without becoming ill. Can the hardy personality survive stress better than others? The "Hardy Personality Type" is disposed toward *commitment* (versus alienation), *control* (versus powerless-

ness), and *challenge* (versus threat) (Kobasa, Hilker, and Maddi 1979; Maddi 1980).

For a person to encounter highly stressful situations and still remain healthy, he must believe in and become aware of himself. The individual must believe that one can control and transform events and must perceive change as an opportunity or challenge instead of regarding it as a threat. When an individual experiences a stressful incident, he is able to energize and become exhilarated instead of worrying and becoming debilitated.

Hundreds of programs, ranging from relaxation to meditation, teach the public techniques for coping with stress. Kobasa's work on existential psychotherapy seeks to transform the individual's outlook and actions so that he is able to assimilate incidents in his experience by making decisions for himself and believing that change is an opportunity for personal growth and human fulfillment.

Nature of the person's value system

How then does a person deal with stress in the environment? The pioneering work of psychologist Walter B. Cannon (1932) describes the doctrine of homeostasis as the means by which the body, using hormonal feedback, preserves a state of equilibrium despite environmental stressors. The cybernetic theory or systems control of occupational stress explains how an individual maintains stabilization concomitantly within the organism and its environment (Ashby 1954, 1966). Because individuals must learn to cope with different stressors in the work environment (Cooper and Payne 1978), the latter theory can help explain time, information, and feedback (Shibutani 1968), a more comprehensive portrayal of the P-E interaction.

> *Temporal factors are crucial, and manifold, in research on human stress. . . . [However,] little consideration has been given to such temporal factors in theory or in research. . . . Time may be one of the most important and most neglected parameters of the problem* (McGrath 1970, p. 23).

> *The focus on information underscores the key notion that information mediates the person-environment relationship. The idea of feedback recognizes that coping*

behavior is purposeful, directed by knowledge of its previous effects. These factors are central to an understanding of stress. Moreover, they are equally applicable to the stress phenomena studied both by physiologists and social scientists (Cummings and Cooper 1979, p. 397).

This perspective focuses on the processes of stress, threat, strain, and adjustment that define and make operative the specific aspects of the P-E fit. Stress and threat refer to the external (environmental) factors disturbing the individual's preferred steady state. Stress represents present conditions in the environment; threat represents factors that could affect the individual's future. Strain is the immediate effect, the disruption within the individual. Adjustment refers to the individual's subsequent behavior to reduce those strains or maintain equilibrium. Usually the literature on occupational stress lacks a distinction between strain (immediate effects, such as dissatisfaction with the job) and adjustment (a person's response, such as curtailed aspirations).

Research suggests that individuals differ widely in their preferences for work. To find out individuals' preferences within the setting of the job requires knowledge of the individual's preferential hierarchy of work values. Cummings and Cooper (1979), in their research on the cybernetic theory of occupational stress, underscore the employee's hierarchy of values and tolerance for disequilibrium within the various work elements.

Values are beliefs that are anchored deeply within a person. An individual develops a hierarchy of values through his identification with parents, teachers, and peers, and through the totality of life experiences. Discovering that one's values are no longer acceptable or finding out that one must act against one's beliefs can summon stressful situations. If, for example, one disagrees with the objectives of a new college curriculum based on the back to basics movement, this value conflict may cause stress. Whenever beliefs are in discord, major distress can occur.

College instructors consistently experience lack of control over time, lack of material resources, and lack of communication. Educators often feel they are victims of situational stress and have little or no control over such factors.

Declining enrollments, dismissal of staff, and reassignments are just a few of the stressful situations and tasks administrators confront. Decreased authority and status, low salaries because of financial constraints, and an emphasis on accountability and evaluation create feelings of powerlessness among educators. No wonder they are the prime target of burnout!

Factors in the Work Environment
Considerable attention has been focused on the physical, social, and organizational factors that contribute to job stress, and the relationship between environmental stress and burnout has been researched to some extent. Certain specific factors in the work environment contribute to stress and thus may lead to burnout: role dynamics, responsibility, occupation, job satisfaction, career paths, and the organization itself.

Role dynamics

How does one define the character of an organization—or of an institution of learning? Perhaps the best way to define it is by identifying the influence the members have on its organization. How do members behave within the organization? Institutions acquire very special characteristics—one might even call it behavior. They behave according to how their members impose selectivity, restriction, persistence, and other paraphernalia of organizational practice to maintain and justify their influence. The organization thus becomes totally dependent on the roles its members choose to perform. As each member does his part, the organization becomes more complex and more specialized, conforming to the interdependence of its organizational role. Out of conformity stem the components of this human and technological organization, for all related functions must serve the institution's overall goal. "To bring that plan to life requires only the appropriate behavior of people as members of organizations. In that requirement, however, lie most of the weakness of modern organizations and most of the frustrations of their leaders" (Kahn et al. 1981, p. 5).

Research on role conflict and role ambiguity shares a common goal: to understand the effects of the environment on the individual's physical and mental health. Here the environment should be viewed as the formal organization or group to which the individual belongs. The character of the organization affects the individual's emotional state and behavior.

An organization depends on the activities of its members. Thus, each member plays a role within the pattern of the organization. To analyze the impact of an organization upon an individual, the members' role behavior should be studied as it affects the individual. Roles selected by those members coming in direct contact with each other are labeled "role set." Members constantly influence and regulate individual behavior in agreement with their own role expectations. Members of a role set are called "role senders."

Within an organization, one can find many instances of undefined expectations. The same is true for institutions of higher education. Nebulous perspectives lead to role ambiguity and role conflict, which in turn create problems of adjustment. How one faces adjustments depends on the individual personality and one's relationships with other members of the role set. Both influences affect the role sender's behavior toward himself and monitor the individual's response to ambiguity and conflict (Kahn et al. 1981).

When role conflict is present, one can infer that several members of the role set presume different role expectations for the focal individual. Varied expectations pressure the individual into digressive forms of behavior. The individual can experience psychological conflict when these role pressures give rise to the role forces within him (Kahn et al. 1964).

Role conflict takes several forms. *Inter-sender* conflict occurs when members of a role set send conflicting expectations to the focal person. *Person-role* conflict occurs when role performance conflicts with an individual's values. *Intra-sender* conflict occurs when contradictory expectations are sent from one sender to another. *Inter-role* conflict occurs when the focal person has two conflicting roles (for example, parent and teacher). Other forms of conflict may develop from these four basic types, such as *role overload,* a prevalent form of conflict in industrial organizations (Kahn et al. 1981, p. 20). Role overload occurs when an individual is expected to perform a wide variety of tasks within a limited time. Kahn (1978) divides role overload into qualitative overload—things that are too difficult to do—and quantitative overload—too many things to do.

Kahn et al. (1964) identified role ambiguity as the second organizational stress factor. Role ambiguity occurs when the required information needed for appropriate performance of a role in a given situation is missing. If the focal person is to conform to the expectations dictated by the members of his role set, then the responsibilities, requirements, and explanations of what is his place within the organization should be clearly communicated to him. This information is required for personal assurance. Such communication will allow the person to know how he should behave to satisfy his personal needs and to protect his values and which behaviors are common to people within the organization. Ambiguity may result if the correct information is not transmitted to the focal person because it is incomplete or insufficient.

Role conflict involves a change in the focal individual's behavior as he is pressured by members of the role set. While the person is trying to maintain some equilibrium in his job, pressure and additional forces threaten his stability, and conflict thus strikes him.

Several investigations have uncovered role conflicts in organizations, which seem to have the potential for disturbing individuals who are exposed to them. Different people vary in their tolerance for role conflict, and some of the personality correlates of this tolerance are known. Usually role conflict is associated with loss of morale, low productivity, and other deleterious effects, leading to symptoms of burnout (Biddle 1979). For this reason, researchers have interpreted role conflict as an important problem that organizations must resolve.

Evidence indicates that role ambiguity is a source of unhappiness among individuals within an organization (Kahn et al. 1964). Katz (1968) contends, however, that some "autonomy" must be provided for employees if they are to solve the daily, shifting problems of their work. But it is not always certain under what circumstances the individual will extend his role or resent the additional structure (Biddle 1979).

Role overload occurs when an individual is faced with a complex role set. People experience stress when faced with too many roles (Coser and Coser 1974; Goode 1960; Merton 1957; Slater 1963; Snoek 1966). It is assumed that individuals have but limited time and energy and that they become distressed when too many demands are placed on them. Although human energy does not seem finite in any simple sense, people at times take on additional roles in which they become stressed, even though they are truly interested and motivated.

In summary, role dynamics apply to institutions of higher education, just as they do to other types of organizations. Colleges and universities comprise the patterns and conforming actions of their faculties and administrators. Hence, the role of each individual member in the institution consists of the part he or she plays in the complete pattern of action.

Responsibility

French and Caplan (1970) hypothesized that specific types of stress at work bring about specific changes in risk factors. For example, an individual under pressure may smoke heavily and his blood pressure and level of cholesterol rise. Responsibility can be another type of stress, because it affects a person physically by increasing his or her risk of coronary attack. It is important to note, however, that merely being responsible is not as important as feeling responsible for the welfare of other people, as is the case with teachers. In addition, being responsible for work-related tasks that involve equipment rather than human beings would probably not increase the risk of coronary attack (Wardwell, Hyman, and Bahnson 1964). In the educator's world, one of the antecedents of burnout is the assumption that students do not learn because teachers do not teach. Although it is false, that premise has become the basis of unrealistic expectations shared by the public, thus causing "frustration, guilt, and sense of failure" among many teachers at all levels of the educational system (Pines, Aronson, and Kafry 1981).

Another reason for the emotional and physiological stress of teachers is the daily confrontation with unmotivated and uninterested students who enter college without the necessary maturity to succeed. Because students do not have the required skills in speaking, reading, and writing, instructors must teach minimal skills. Although this untraditional student has been called "the new student" (Cross 1971), it is truly the faculty of the eighties who should be called "the new faculty." They have had to prepare psychologically and emotionally to master their new role as paternal educator, because many college students still have to be led by the hand and guided in the management of their own learning. The additional feeling of responsibility for other human beings' welfare thus creates stress in college teachers who have been trained with traditional high standards at graduate school. As a helping profession, teaching promotes the danger of burnout and exhaustion because teaching especially demands giving emotionally of oneself to others.

Occupation

Although most college administrators have been faculty members at one point or another, the occupations of administrator and instructor are characterized by different types of stress. The job of administrator entails one type of responsibility, the job of instructor another. Various forms of job stress might affect risk factors in different ways.

The nature of occupational differences between administrator and instructor can have a different relationship to burnout. Persons who are burnt out tend to differ in disposition and temperament from those who are not. The Type A personality, as previously mentioned, is more prone to coronary attack because such an individual is characterized as being aggressive, hostile, ambitious, conscious of time, impatient, pressured, and engaged in multiple activities. If the variable for the need of social approval is added, then the individual can suffer even greater strain under pressure, which usually happens because the person is greatly influenced by the criticisms of others in his social (work) environment.

Personality variables might have some effect on coronary heart disease through several channels.

Personality may influence heart disease via occupational choice. For example, the coronary personality may be more likely to seek out the risk administrative job rather than the job of engineer or scientist (equivalent to college professor). And, perhaps, the coronary personality who finds himself in an engineering job takes steps to move into a more administrative job. Another channel through which personality may have its effect is in mediating the relationship between one's occupation and the stress one experiences in that occupation. . . . To give an illustration a manager when objectively overloaded may be more likely to experience subjective overload because he is a Type A personality. [The third channel is] while job stress may cause changes in risk factors such as cholesterol and number of cigarettes smoked, such changes are perhaps more likely to occur if the person is Type A rather than Type B (French and Caplan 1970, p. 386).

Day by day the administrator tries to cope with the different kinds of pressures that occur. As pressures mount, they gradually overcome the administrator, who eventually experiences a sense of helplessness because he no longer has the power or autonomy to act. A former burnt-out administrator explains how the social forces behind the occupation of administrator can lead to burnout.

Living in the center of the cyclone, with no safe ground anywhere and in a chronic state of "information overload" and "psychological crowding," leads inexorably to physiological and behavioral deterioration among even the strongest and most resourceful human beings— just as physical crowding has been shown to do with lower species (Vash 1980, p. 4).

Job satisfaction
Role conflict and role ambiguity in different types of occupations significantly affect job satisfaction and personal stress (Schuler, Aldag, and Brief 1977). Burke (1976) found that job satisfaction is related to four occupational stresses: excess of responsibility, perceiving oneself as unqualified, excessive workload, and lack of input in decision making. Individuals with Type A behavior experience great job conflicts and dissatisfaction (Howard, Cunningham, and Rechnitger 1977). Job satisfaction can be related to coronary heart disease (French and Caplan 1970; Sales 1969a). Subjects conditioned to overload and to underload demonstrated significant differences with regard to job satisfaction; the most dissatisfied showed an increase in cholesterol, thus suggesting the possibility of coronary heart

disease. Studies building upon Sales's work at the University of Michigan contend that the risk of developing coronary heart disease depends on whether the subject is motivated to work for a salary or for prestige (extrinsic rewards) or simply for enjoyment (intrinsic rewards). Working for extrinsic rewards indicates a higher likelihood of coronary heart disease than working for intrinsic rewards. "Organizational roles, whether overloading or not, exert their most harmful effects upon those organizational members who experience the lowest job satisfaction" (Sales 1969b, p. 325).

Findings on the influence of work overload as a source of stress among faculty and administrators demonstrate that faculty suffered from low self-esteem because they were unable to complete a high-quality task (French, Tupper, and Mueller 1965). Administrators also suffered from low self-esteem but for a different reason: They had to complete a certain amount of work in a given time, even if it meant not doing their best.

The broad array of studies presents considerable evidence that certain psychological and social factors indicate a tendency toward coronary heart disease (Jenkins 1976). Regarding factors that contribute to burnout, "burnout is best understood in terms of social and situational sources of job-related stress" (Maslach 1978, p. 115).

Job satisfaction in higher education is an important variable that should be researched further because studies demonstrate that well-satisfied instructors develop more concern for students' achievement. The recent high level of interest in job satisfaction at colleges and universities is primarily the result of a shift in Americans' outlook: We expect more from our work environment than merely a salary (Special Task Force 1973). Accomplishing an important job ensures personal identity and reflects a sense of well-being.

Are stress and job satisfaction related? Pressure and gratification are closely related. When stress is functional, it can act as a stimulus to growth, thus enabling the individual to achieve a new balance. If a person responds to this stimulus, he grows and thus gains job satisfaction. College faculty carry heavy workloads; they are expected to teach, counsel, research, lecture, publish, participate in community service, become appointed to important committees, and prepare new curricula. All these tasks—or the necessity to perform them simultaneously—can cause stress. Most faculty usually perform their best under this kind of pressure. Surely when such tasks are fulfilled, they engender feelings of pride and job satisfaction. When stress is thus an impetus to growth, it serves as a motivator for operating at one's highest capabilities. Teachers should not avoid stress, but they should learn to handle their stress constructively to serve their purposes and avoid burnout.

Career paths

During a lifetime, chains of varying experiences are linked to represent the familiar concept of career. To the ancient Greeks, the term meant a running race.

> *Whether stable or mobile, the career represents an orga-*
> *nized or patterned path taken by an individual across*
> *time and space. The career then is simply a series of*
> *separate but related experiences and adventures through*
> *which a person passes during a lifetime. It can be long*
> *or short and of course an individual can pursue multiple*
> *careers either in rough sequence or at the same time*
> (Van Maanen 1977, p. 1).

Van Maanen explains further that the most meaningful aspect of an individual's career is the importance it has in his or her entire life. How significant is one's career in comparison to all other aspects of life?

At one time a person's career was determined by the parents' occupation. In this world of *gemeinschaft,* children could picture themselves similar to their parents, working and growing older in a particular community, following a particular social order of mores, folkways, and religion. The nineteenth century saw a transformation from *gemeinschaft* to *gesellschaft,* however—the world in which one strives for his own fortune, thus developing individualism. The world of work thus becomes "the principle around which the individual organizes his or her life [and makes] choices that affect the course [of his or her life]" (Van Maanen 1977, p. 1), and the individual finds a list of choices with titles that offer a variety of careers. Hence, the ties between organizational context and the involved person continue to be topics of research for the dis-

When stress is . . . an impetus to growth, it serves as a motivator for operating at one's highest capabilities.

covery of new clues in one's life course and identity within the institutional compound.

Psychological outlook and attitude normally change during an individual's life cycle. Therefore, becoming a member of an organization for the purposes of work cannot mean stagnation for the individual because both the person and the organization change with time. The individual progresses with age, experience, and knowledge, and the organization changes to keep pace with time. Thus, progression is continuously revised and negotiated at different stages, creating meaningful changes.

It is through the acquisition of experiences over a lifetime that an individual gains his or her identity. Thus, personal identity is achieved through perpetual transitions that come as a result of experiences during a lifetime. To understand the individual, one must have a notion of that person's past and possible future. Observing a person within a career includes viewing his patterns of involvement in the workplace and his personal experiences. In past years, the focus of research would have been on issues of identity, but now psychologists and educators who study life cycles are more interested in adult development and more recently "mid-career crisis." This interest is no other than the reviewing, reappraising, and redefining of the total life situation, including the status of one's work and personal life. Mid-career crisis is a turning point, when a person is supposed to be at his or her career's peak and has acquired professional security and distinction. It is a reassessment of a possible life structure with new choices for testing and a need to plan and make use of the future more wisely. In part, it is a reappraisal of the past.

What have I done with my life? What do I really get from and give to my wife, children, friends, work, community—and self? What is it I truly want for myself and others? What are my central values and how am I using (or wasting) them? What have I done with my early Dream and what do I want with it now? Can I live in a way that combines my life structure—how suitable for the self, how viable in the world, and how shall I change it to provide a better basis for the future? (Levinson 1978, p. 192).

Erikson's epigenetic theory of the stages of human life, which remodels the interaction of a person's biological, psychological, and social factors, has served as the basis for other comprehensive accounts of developmental stages throughout a lifetime or a career (Levinson 1978; Sheehy 1974; Weathersby and Tarule 1980). The significance of this theory in higher education has been related to works on faculty development and job satisfaction. As such, however, with the exception of Hodgkinson (1974), who applies the concept of Erikson's early work on generativity, the phenomenon has received little attention in higher education. Hodgkinson acknowledges the significance of generativity by describing the psychological problems and job pressures of faculty and administrators that develop at different stages of adulthood. By following Levinson's developmental stages, he relates the concept to "mid-career crisis" among higher education personnel from the ages of 39 to 43.

Before reaching the midlife transition, the potential for personal and professional conflicts is considerable. Hodgkinson explains the deprived psychological situation of faculty during the Settling Down period.

During this period most faculty between ages 30 and 35 are still mainly dependent on others because of the slowness with which higher education rewards ability and competence by allowing mobility through the status structure of faculty committees, etc. In many sectors of business and industry, talent and performance are rewarded more rapidly, and the rewards are more relevant to the person (1974, p. 268).

The Becoming One's Own Person stage for faculty (ages 35 to 39) is the time when the drive is toward tenure.

Particularly in institutions in which the criteria for tenure are vague or perhaps even schizophrenic (in the sense of pressure on the faculty members of small institutions to teach as well as [and] to produce as much research as counterparts at a major university), the potential for personal and marital conflicts is considerable in this age. The person simply has too many different places to be at the same time, and in a number of experimental colleges particularly the 35-year-old faculty member may be torn between five or six equally important and worthwhile tasks, some related to teaching, some to research, and some to his own family. Some faculty members begin to show physical and neurological deterioration over this conflict during their late thirties (pp. 268–69).

For administrators aged 35 to 39,

. . . this period [sees] the drive for the "top job," [and] family conflicts are more likely to break out in administrative than faculty households. The administrator is also pushed in too many directions and must be responsible to too many different individuals and groups, and often the family gets shunted aside (p. 269).

"Middlescence" (ages 39 to 43), is the stage when most people are apt to think seriously about the matters of life and death, the dreams that could have been and were not, the realities of today, and the future for the other half of one's life. During these years, Hodgkinson says,

many faculty members feel obliged to revise downward The Dream developed in the Getting-into-the-Adult-World period. This may mean that the status of the institution with which he or she is associated may be reassessed; one's own status among one's peers may be revised downward as well as the sense of one's own autonomy, influence, and power. For some, this period represents the last chance to get out of teaching and into something else, and many individuals take advantage of that opportunity during these years. Also, if the faculty member has been successful in his drive to Become His Own Man, he must calculate from the perspective of full professor, age 40, with tenure, the reward structure for the next 25 years before retirement. For most faculty members this is a fairly grim prospect, as most institutions do not have much of a reward structure except economic, for the intervening years (p. 270).

And he adds:

Divorce and suicide rates are relatively high for the population as a whole during these years, and I suspect that college and university faculty members are no exception (p. 270).

Midlife for the administrator signifies "the possible shattering of the 'grand illusion,' meaning that [he] realizes that [he] has much less power, autonomy, and visibility than [he] expected in The Dream" (p. 271). After so many years of working with people, the administrator realizes that he has made more enemies than friends and that he will never become a dean, much less a president. It is a very painful stage for the administrator because upper-echelon administrators are usually selected on the basis of "irrelevant social niceties."

According to Hodgkinson, for those who survive middlescence, the remaining years until 50 should be a significant period in the individual's personal life and work. It is the phase when the faculty member shows institutional pride through enjoying his role of mentor, orchestrating life with meaningful and productive academic and social events, and selecting projects in the local community. As for the administrator, this stage is one for greater enjoyment and personal satisfaction as a mentor for junior administrators, faculty, and students, because by this point one has developed greater confidence and a particular style of management. Often, the administrator teaches at least one course, which provides additional intellectual interest.

Generativity means a concern with the next generation. As described by Erikson, it includes procreativity, productivity, and creativity. Generativity has eight stages, and a particular vital strength is ascribed to each stage. Beginning with *hope* at infancy, these strengths arise and develop through psychosexual stages and psychosocial conflicts. The second stage is the age of early childhood and *will,* while during the third stage, the play age, the child gains *purpose.* The fourth stage, when the child reaches school age, brings *competence.* In adolescence, there is *fidelity,* in young adulthood *love,* in adulthood *care.* The last stage, old age, represents *wisdom.* To visualize epigenesis contextually, Erikson explains:

> *Thus . . . , each item has its critical time of decisive un-folding along the diagonal, while it already existed in some form at earlier stages under the dominance of the then critical conflicts, and it will be revised and renewed in all subsequent stages in relation to the items then to become dominant* (Erikson and Erikson 1981, p. 252).

One can clearly follow the stages and the "syntonic" items (making for development) and the "dystonic" ones (causing human conflicts) as they continue up the diagonal (years) and add their particular character to the entire life pattern of the individual (Erikson and Erikson 1981).

The stage of middle adulthood is the stage of generativity, and it raises several questions: How and how long can faculty remain generative in a low-growth economy, increased tempo of living, accelerated rate of change, career-related depressions, and tension-producing phenomena? Stress seems to be activated by the nation's economic situation. Thus, the problem of retrenchment in higher education has created a situation that brings little or no economic rewards in teaching. In turn, the situation has brought about enervating feelings and bitterness for the generation of faculty for whom academia represents life. Today they are haunted by a question: What remains after teaching? The answer has several components.

> *. . . Most of us do not even admit to ourselves that we are facing a major crisis. The admission of a fear of sameness, of there being nothing more in our profession to achieve except that which we have reached, the mere accumulative process—one more review, one more article, one more book—is frightening and psychologically so debilitating that its acceptance alone is enough to deny its probable existence. Coupled with it are concrete fears as well: fear for smaller raises in economically hard times, fear of being fired from our jobs when the academic market is closed, and the fear of being laughed at by colleagues on the up-side of the crisis years. These are all powerful inhibitors of getting the truth revealed* (Volgyes 1982, p. 10).

This phenomenon of teacher despair can be attributed not only to midlife crisis or burnout but also to a period that makes this generation feel like the slice of ham in a sandwich, trapped in the middle of two generations, dissimilar from both the previous one and the successive one (Volgyes 1982).

But the problem is what to do about the crisis, for becoming a community of "nongenerative" scholars as well as candidates for burnout has dangerous consequences. Because we concentrate so vigorously on the pressures of our environment, we are risking our sense of common purpose that is to guide the next generation (Knefelkamp 1980). Generative institutions are

> . . . *a link between the past and the future and so are involved with scholarship as a way of allowing the young scholar to be a part of the intellectual history of his field and feel a sense of confidence about contributing to the field's future* (Knefelkamp 1980, p. 16).

Among several alternatives, Knefelkamp (1980) presents the P-E fit model as one in which individual development is possible through the interaction of the person and the environment. The individual will likely be more productive when the environment fits his needs.

Generativity, the stage of caring for the welfare of others, is a basic concept in the psychosocial development of adults. Only recently, however, has the literature on developmental patterns between the ages of 18 and 55 burgeoned. The period of the midlife crisis is the stage during one's life when major changes in behavior and career take place. Examining these changes will provide insight on how to foster a satisfying and productive life in middle adulthood.

Middle age, according to Levinson,

> . . . *involves greater responsibility, perspective, and judgment. A person in this era must be able to care for younger and older adults, to exercise authority creatively, to transcend the youthful extremes of shallow conformity and impulsive rebelliousness. The moderate midlife decrease in biological capacity must be counterbalanced by an increased psychosocial capacity. In countless intellectual, emotional, moral, esthetic, mana-*

gerial, and reparative ways, the middle-age must help in maintaining and developing the culture (1978, p. 329).

Regarding work, Levinson explains that a man in the midlife transition recognizes that he will never advance into becoming that imagined "writer, educator, political leader, or violin maker."

He will never rise to the level he sought in the military, the corporation or the church. He will fall far short of his early Dream. This is a crucial turning point. He may decide to continue in his present job, doing work that is increasingly routine and humiliating. He may change to another job, or another occupation, that offers more challenge and satisfaction. Or he may reduce his interest in work, performing well enough to keep employed but investing himself more in other aspects of life such as the family or leisure (1978, p. 220).

Only recently has an awareness of developmental cycles been applied to studies related to topics on faculty development in higher education. Monies allocated for professional growth programs at community colleges triggered a wealth of research on faculty members' evaluation, accountability, job satisfaction, characteristics, etc. Most research has been deficient in perceiving the personal needs and values of faculty and administrators, however. More recently, some papers have exposed new findings on motivation and behavior at work (see Kanter 1978, for example). Kanter says higher education administrators must "put their own houses in order or their ability to operate effectively as educators may be seriously impaired" (1978, p. 7). Contrasting two groups of academics, she calls one group "moving," those who manage to climb up the professional ladder, and the other "stuck," those who lack the opportunity and are likely "to either become psychic dropouts . . . or to actually dream of escape from the organization into some realm" (p. 7). The stuck individual shows characteristics equivalent to those of a burnt out person.

The stuck . . . tend to think less well of themselves and tend to underrate and devalue their skills and abilities. This applies whether they are in job categories that have

*always been stuck, by design, or whether they got stuck
after the experience of mobility and began to question
whether they really possess the right kinds of skills for
success. The stuck, therefore, are much less likely to
perceive themselves as skilled, to make their skills or
abilities known, or to feel that they can carry out assignments for which they do not already have the experience; the stuck are unlikely to give the organization any
indication that they deserve to do more than is de-
manded by their current position* (Kanter 1978, p. 6).

Maslach's definitions of burnout aptly relate to Kanter's
description of the stuck individual:

- *A progressive loss of idealism, energy, and purpose
  experienced by people in the helping professions as a
  result of the conditions of their work.*
- *A malaise of the spirit. A loss of will. An inability to
  mobilize interests and capabilities.*
- *A process in which a professional's attitudes and behavior change in negative ways in response to job
  strain.*
- *A debilitating psychological condition resulting from
  work-related frustrations, which results in lower employee productivity and morale* (1982b, pp. 30–31).

These definitions of burnout all indicate that stuckness and
burnout share the following aspects:

1. Burnout/stuckness occur in individuals.
2. Burnout/stuckness refer to feelings, attitudes, and
   motives of the person involved.
3. Burnout/stuckness can be described as a process.
4. Burnout/stuckness can become a negative experience
   for the individual because they now involve a dysfunction that has become a permanent and negative
   condition stemming from the individual's lack of self-
   confidence for each job expectation.

Baldwin identifies five career stages for faculty at liberal
arts colleges, which he defines according to the following
academic ranks:

1. *Assistant professors in the first three years of full-
   time college teaching*

*2. Assistant professors with more than three years of
      college teaching experience*
3. Associate professors
4. Full professors more than five years from retirement
5. Full professors within five years of retirement (1979,
      p. 16).

*In general, associate professors are satisfied with their
career progress to date. Yet occasionally they are
nagged by the fear that they have reached a dead end,
that their career has plateaued, and that they have no-
where to go professionally* (p. 19).

Full professors more than five years from retirement, however,

*. . . have reached a watershed in their careers . . . . They
are faced with a choice between stagnation and diversifi-
cation. During this period, continuing full professors
sometimes question the value of their vocation. . . . Advanced faculty members who fail to "branch out" can
fall victim to career inertia. Limited opportunities for
professional growth may lead to disillusionment or depression, which can very likely affect the performance of
these professors* (p. 19).

The midlife career crisis has obvious implications for the
tenured faculty who may suffer from stress because of the
immobility that occurs in a time of few opportunities and
little or no incentive to stay on the job. Many suffer tedium
in teaching and experience feelings of incompetence as the
result of the lack of motivation or rewards. Others leave
academe before burning out and thus benefit from midcareer transition. Many colleges, however, inherit the unmotivated, uninspired, and possibly bitter breed of faculty.
They are the individuals experiencing midlife crisis whose
symptoms are similar to those of burnout: feelings of emp-
tiness, disillusionment, and deep despair (Pines, Aronson,
and Kafry 1981).

What alternatives can help the development of the mid-
career faculty? Patton (1981) suggests three ways: (1) a systematic approach to long-term planning in which faculty
prepare a three-year professional plan that is up dated an-

nually to help outline improvement in all departments, thus allowing faculty to have control over their professional careers; (2) intrauniversity visiting professorships in which faculty are awarded one month's summer salary plus an academic year free of departmental tasks to take courses, team-teach, or engage in interdisciplinary work; (3) the exchange of faculty with other universities (p. 5). Perhaps another alternative would be to honor a colleague by offering him the opportunity to present a series of lectures. It holds true that when "the ideas of education [are] again discussed and intellectualism . . . [becomes] the hallmark of our trade . . . there will be, once again, life after teaching for student and professors alike" (Volgyes 1982, p. 11).

The organization

The university is referred to as a permanent association, comprised of a group of individuals who have joined efforts toward a common objective and formed an institution with specific governing rules and regulations for membership. To pursue the association's goals, the founders authorize a governing body to establish a bureaucracy. It is the bureaucracy of a university that administers work for the association.

A tendency exists to visualize the organization of the university in "bureaucratic manager-subordinate terms." This view fails to consider that universities are distinguished for their major functions of development, criticism, and evaluation of ideas. They should be protected and carried out by emphasizing academic freedom for the faculty. The university is an association, and the faculty are *members* of that association, not mere employees of the university (Jacques 1976).

The most important people in colleges and universities are the faculty members. They are the essential ingredient for several reasons. Theirs is the primary responsibility for conducting the academic program of the institution. And the academic program is the basic reason for having colleges and universities.

In addition to their role of conducting the educational operations of institutions of higher learning, the faculty members are the people in closest and most continuous contact with the students. They are key people who meet

Many [tenured faculty] . . . experience feelings of incompetence as the result of lack of motivation or rewards.

with the students in classes, laboratories, seminars, and other learning situations. They are the core of the college or university that is expected to remain on campus and give continuity over the years to the institution (Bornheimer, Burns, and Dunke 1973, preface).

The fear of negative sanctioning should not exist among the faculty. Life tenure should be a policy so that faculty feel free and secure to develop and express the ideas of society.

> *. . . The idea of academic freedom [is] that a teacher or professor is free to teach or profess, without interference, any and all aspects of that course or subject in which he is professionally qualified. In addition, it is expected that a faculty member will have all the rights and the responsibilities of any other citizen to express himself off campus on any and all subjects without reference to his position or profession. However, it goes without saying that society expects persons of prominence in the professions to exercise restraint in terms of decorum and delivery in making public pronouncements* (Bornheimer, Burns, and Dunke 1973, p. 18).

The idea of a bureaucratic organization should not be imposed upon the university. The idea of manager-subordinate is totally inconsistent with the idea of a university. Sad to say, however, this form of governance is steadily creeping into the many windows of the university—as in the academic department where the department head is thought of as manager and held accountable for the work of the faculty in the department, including the research ideas they develop. Such a relationship between managerial control and the development of ideas is death to academic freedom (Jacques 1976, p. 344). The collegial functioning of the department should be monitored and coordinated by a chairperson who can also appoint new staff. It is the faculty of the department who can determine teaching, course requirements, and curricula, observing the university's policies and collegial ethics.

Department staff are familiar with collegial duties and are well aware that students are free individuals who come to the university pursuing the education of their choice. Integrating the university into the community and rendering its resources to serve humanity are two of its most outstanding missions. Already in this age of information, we are perceiving the university as the place where "learning happens across an interdependent curriculum" (Wallin 1983, p. 7). These ideas are sometimes misguided, misinterpreted, or forgotten, however, and we tend to brand the university in bureaucratic, hierarchical terms, such as boss, employee, and customer or consumer of education. Once the faculty become regarded as salespersons of education or employees within a manager-subordinate bureaucracy, students come to be regarded as customers as well. The teacher-student relationship is then completely lost. The focus is no longer on the search for knowledge but instead on an economic priority. One way of overcoming this situation is by providing tenure for faculty. Under those conditions, the professional relationship between faculty and administrator can become an operative one without managerial interference or control but within institutional policy and central monitoring.

Granting of tenure is the mode of admission to the university association. Teaching staff without tenure will not be found to have the status of members of the university; they are its employees (perhaps on probation as association members) in the way that members of the administrative staff employed by the university are employees (Jacques 1976, p. 60).

The tenure debate becomes one of the major sources of frustration among academics.

Hence, the university, through internal resistance, is pressured by a confusion of goals and therefore plagued by an institutional disease, "burnout," that stems from the stressful institutional climate contributing to the paranoia of both faculty and decision makers. Stress in the organizational environment damages faculty members' performance no matter what the cause may be.

When the stress is severe faculty resign, and they say they feel pushed out by an organizational climate which neither recognizes nor supports them as professionals or as individuals of personal worth. But when stress in the organization simply rankles and irritates, when it leads professors to wonder if anybody cares about teaching at all, then one might predict that members of the organization have the feeling they are working at cross purposes (Peters and Mayfield 1982, p. 105).

We may note, therefore, that universities are threatened by bureaucratization.

Describing how an individual experiences and relates to the organization throughout his career-moves may serve to discern a process of socialization in the period the organization has maximum influence. On the other hand, one can also follow the span of faculty performance. What can the college professor expect of the institution once he or she becomes a member of that organization? How can he guide his decisions concerning mobility within the organization? Do these data serve to enlighten the relationship between the individual and the organization, especially when the university in the modern world seems to be functioning at a vastly different pace from what most faculty originally anticipated? Preparing for the future and having knowledge of the institution's expectations will aid faculty in avoiding friction with the administration. Faculty want to be part of the restructuring of goals and definitions. Cognizant of the evaluation process and new design of higher education, the faculty as members of the association can pool their efforts toward integration of the university community.

An individual invents and constructs different selves for different performances and different roles. During this process of socialization, one internalizes rules, norms, values, attitudes, and behaviors. Patterns become automatic and part of the individual. With respect to each role demand, the person develops aspirations, expectations, attributes, and behaviors to be able to fulfill roles at least at minimum capacity. As a result of this process of career socialization, changes occur to the different adult social selves with little change to the basic personality structure. With every new demand, the individual uses attributes and skills from his or her repertoire to construct or reconstruct his or her roles. Strengths and weaknesses are defined from the person's combination of established beliefs and attitudes and their flexibility to adapt to the different social selves (Schein 1971).

The dynamics of a career allow the individual to move upward, around, and inward, which seems to be the motion in every career. Within the university, however, it is very common to move upward without moving inward or around. Such is the situation in the case of the scholar who becomes a full professor but is never given any administrative power in the university and thus feels excluded from the central functioning of the university. To have power and access to information, the individual must move inward or toward the nucleus of the organization. This move may provide rank, but it often deprives the assistant or associate dean of the kind of power associated with the position. Such is the case with women who become assistants and associates but never deans. Most women and minorities are confined to a narrow range of positions and institutions (Moore 1983, p. 6). As a whole, women are promoted more often than men, but their promotions are smaller and thus they reside in lower positions in the corporate hierarchy (Bridgwater 1983, p. 16). The old wives' tale that women are not often employed as administrators because they are more emotional and less rational than men or are less committed to their careers, however, was proven otherwise (Tung 1980). Tung compared the occupational stress of male and female educational administrators to determine whether their profiles differed significantly. Findings demonstrated that female administrators experienced substantially lower levels of self-perceived occupational stress than their male counterparts. Professional women did not differ significantly from men in the experience of tedium (Pines and Kafry 1981). This finding is very significant, because women reported fewer rewards than men and more pressures and stress in the work environment than men. In addition, tedium was lower for women who maintained strong social support systems. Burnout among women was shown to be less severe at institutions where feelings were expressed openly, work tasks were shared, and solid or satisfying personal relationships prevailed.

What about support and concern for middle managers at a college? They are the managers who have limited mobility in a stratified hierarchical setting. How can their performances be rewarded to avoid symptoms of "stuckness," especially when few opportunities for advancement and low job satisfaction are so obvious? Can their self-esteem be enhanced when there is such a vague change for professional growth? Can burnout be avoided? Scott (1979) suggests the development of new models of mobility and growth in which employees at all levels must be valued, productive, and satisfied. His advice is to follow the trail of the "reinsman"—self-confident, challenging, and ready to confront the unexpected (p. 21).

Institutional factors do influence the level of stress. The administrative stamp of approval on certain academic tasks is not necessarily assurance for faculty of job satisfaction or personal development. The university structure treats faculty like workers and requires them to perform tasks that seem of little interest (Bess 1982). This attitude diminishes institutions' effectiveness and individuals' satisfaction. Administrators refer to faculty as employees because of the two different types of social relation that operate (Pankin 1973) as a consequence of the two structures. Decision makers are structured bureaucratically and hierarchically, contrary to faculty, who interact with each other on an egalitarian basis. Along with this perception of equals, the college professor has acquired an image of high social position on campus and is respected for professional intellectualism and prestige. Many times, faculty are more influential than administrators. They feel their duties go beyond teaching. Responsibilities of research, public service, consulting, and campus governance, among others, expose them to different groups in the community. "High-status" faculty, who are

> . . . accustomed to being treated as high status persons[,] tend soon to believe that they are somehow better than others. Academics tend to believe that they "deserve" some kind of subservience from service personnel (Bess 1982, p. 121).

There is no question that differences in power and status create disadvantages for the institution. Positive relationships with others could buffer the impact of many work and life stressors. Moreover, equality of status could allow for a chance to interact in a social system that provides an adequate environment for possible dialogue and the achievement of personal satisfaction and institutional goals. Lack of social contact, which is a serious psychological stressor, produces feelings of frustration and hopelessness, while failing to provide adequate outlets for feelings.

Bess proposes a new mode of institutional organization in which faculty skills and interests carry out all the academic activities of the entire institution. Task units are set up to meet the aims of both processes (such as research) and clients (such as students); thus, institutional objectives become more efficient and faculty become more satisfied.

Any one of the three components of the organizational design—role structure, power structure, and normative structure—can affect the incidence of staff burnout. Certain role structures tend to influence the severity of staff burnout, such as role conflict and role ambiguity among faculty. Hierarchical decision making can increase burnout among middle managers. Their feelings of low self-concept and low satisfaction are major contributors to stress. The third major component of the organizational design, the normative structure (goals, norms, and ideologies), tends to elicit higher levels of stress, particularly when high expectations meet the failure to receive awaited rewards.

Countless books, courses on college campuses, workshops, and lectures deal with stress management. Recently, the literature, lectures, and conferences are sounding out the word "burnout." The concept of burnout is becoming so familiar that one can hear nurses, social workers, athletes, teachers, and even executives exclaim, "Thank God it's Friday. I'm burnt out!" The word alone implies a devastating outcome (Marrow 1981), such as ashes resulting from fire. Burnout refers to a process that "is often a consequence of an overload of stress." This process is "infectious," because "it can operate on a group level spreading in every direction" (Freudenberger 1981, p. 10). It usually affects the most productive individuals, who as high achievers are slaves of constant professional demands, living at an acutely stressful pace. These bright individuals either learn to cope with their stressful lives or succumb to burnout. "A victim's emotional circuits become increasingly overloaded from constant excessive demands on his or her energy, strength, and resources" (Freudenberger 1981, p. 1).

Reviewing the Symptoms
Reported symptoms range from feeling tired in the morning, which forces one to slow down on the job, to becoming impatient, cynical, nagging, inflexible, or defensive, to experiencing exhaustion accompanied by physical discomforts, possible weight loss, and continued negative attitude. Thinking may be hampered to the point where the individual is unable to concentrate and recall important facts (Freudenberger 1980). Naturally these symptoms do not occur all at once, and many times the individual is not aware of them because "the object of the whole game, of course, is never to show weakness. . . . Rather we may subvert ourselves by working harder, longer and deny even more that we are burning out" (Freudenberger 1981, p. 7).

Can burnout strike a college president? Yes, burnout can have a very special affinity for any executive, whether president, chancellor, or dean. In fact, "like generalized stress, burnout cuts across executive and managerial levels" (Levinson 1981, p. 74). And like the professoriate, the decision maker also believes in the great American dream—that anyone can make it to the top. Hence, even though he is well aware that there are few positions at the top, he continues to strive. Like Darwin, he believes that only the fittest will survive. Sooner or later, however, efforts to reach the top become the unfulfilled Dream for most (Freudenberger 1981). For those who reach the top—college presidents, for example—tasks related to fiscal matters and sources of funding produce the greatest stress (Duea 1981). While executives suffer symptoms of burnout, however, they are still able to be efficient (Levinson 1981). Presidents in middle life, who have been in governance for a number of years, feel "stuck" at the top yet look forward to new "passages" (Vaughan 1982).

Both faculty and administrators have experienced the sense of low ceiling for advancement (Kanter 1978). Those who feel "stuck" are the individuals who give up trying to get ahead, develop physical ailments, and become gripers. The stuck reinforce their own stuckness, thus resulting in a case of burnout (Howard and Downey 1980).

Examining Roots

Sociologically, causes of burnout are attributed to the obvious fast changes in tradition, including new mores, new lifestyles, new family units, and the drug epidemic. To this list, add the modern age of information (Wallin 1983), technology and the computer, economic inflation, herpes and AIDS, the dilemma of nuclear disarmament, and the development of the third world countries. "Now people are wondering how to survive" this turmoil (Freudenberger 1981, p. 4).

What are some of the roots of burnout in academia? Several facets of faculty work experience in academia provide background on the present employment crisis in higher education.

In the present employment crisis, one of the most devastating experiences for a bright, capable person is to experience a sense of failure. Despite everything we know about statistics of employment of PhDs, the individual whose contract is not renewed or who does not receive tenure generally blames herself or himself rather than the system. This penchant for self-destruction among academics is often accentuated by our regrettable habit of judging, and often rejecting, junior faculty after one or three years of teaching and research as though they

[B]urnout can have a . . . special affinity for any executive, whether president, chancellor, or dean.

were finished products off an assembly line, to be ac-
cepted or rejected. It is particularly ironic that educa-
tional institutions treat their most important resource as
ineducable. The institution which can devise a "faculty
development" program in teaching effectiveness to as-
sist junior and senior faculty without threatening either
one with immediate humiliation, death, or destruction
will do a great deal to ensure both good morale gener-
ally and a junior faculty confident of its skills and its fu-
ture, in one institution or another (Lazarus and Tolpin
1979, p. 30).

The junior faculty member is seen struggling to make it
up the career ladder while the senior faculty member remains distant and ensconced in research, although also trying to survive in an unchallenging environment without the
kinds of support needed—economic, political, and cultural—to enable the academics to fulfill their functions ade-
quately. Rewards become fewer, morale lower. The junior
faculty member, if he does not decide to bail out, suffers
like the nomad who wanders from campus to campus and
cannot find refuge. Finally, the miracle happens, and a
teaching position is offered—but alas it comes without security. The race for a position on the tenure track begins
by engaging in teaching, committee work, scholarly writing, and community service. Most likely, the individual encounters many institutional pressures, among them his
peers' criticism of his research (Ladd 1979) and a lack of
support from senior faculty to act as mentors (Lazarus and
Tolpin 1979). The person continues to put a lot of effort
into work as he or she strives for that position on the tenure track. The number of available positions becomes
fewer and fewer. But he believes he is the best and in the
long run knows he will get it. This dream or hope shatters
when reality is not fulfilled. The consequences can be a severe letdown when he realizes he is stuck. And the process
of burnout begins (Freudenberger 1981).
    Can tenure mean so much? Yes, tenure provides the fac-
ulty member with an incentive to grow roots in an institution. It also fosters the myth that faculty will remain dedicated and effective until "death do us part," however. The
probabilities are that some faculty will wither into continued boredom and then feel guilty for not moving on to an-

other, more rewarding job. Others might even become envious of friends who have less expertise and experience but are earning higher salaries in private business. No one wants to keep an unmotivated, resentful faculty, and both the person and the institution will benefit if the individual takes the plunge to deeper and richer waters.

To avert such problems, it is high time faculty severed the umbilical cord that binds them to institutions. Aren't academics the so-called "independent" professionals? It seems they are not. Academics are trained to be dedicated professionals. The traditional Ph.D. program prepares them to be serious-minded, hard workers. Must institutions, however, continue to administer tenure like fine wine, as an antidote to stress? Perhaps it is the best answer for now. Tenure is not only very important for the academics, but it also serves as a bargaining tool for the administration in its dealings with professors (O'Toole 1978).

Members of the higher education community voice their dissatisfaction with academia. Behind each voice is an individual seeking identity, recognition, fulfillment, and meaning in the total academic environment (Knefelkamp 1980). Higher education has joined the rest of society in a period of financial limitation happening so fast that it did not give the American public a chance to adjust to the situation. Thus, it has endangered the influence of the major social institutions of the nation: universities, corporations, private and public enterprises. In general, institutions have become increasingly fragmented as their authority has decreased. One of a university's major roles, which is "to socialize the process of indoctrinating the central values of society," has been weakened (Darrow 1979, p. 13).

This phenomenon of limitations has become personalized, and people from all walks of life are concerned with self-survival. In academia, constraint in the college environment has helped to contribute to tension, confusion, and confrontation among decision makers and faculty and has inhibited personal growth and institutional development.

While the slow economic situation and high inflation give rise to feelings of bitterness, frustration, and alienation in men and women who feel they should be given the opportunity to grow professionally, the entire drama of academia is also in danger of becoming depressingly nongenerative

(Knefelkamp 1980). The scenario for academics is thus plotted with fear and insecurity; it lacks a clear direction for tomorrow.

Identifying Stressors

The novel encounters of the eighties have brought with them new uncertainties and frustrations. The most compelling of these changes have triggered several stress-producing developments among faculty:

> *(1) mandated student and/or peer evaluation, (2) stringent guidelines [that] must be met in order to be promoted in rank or to acquire tenure, (3) increased fear of dismissal due to financial exigency or "dried-up" decreased areas, (4) decreased mobility and job opportunities, (5) inadequate yearly compensation and salary increases, (6) decreased student enrollment leading to inhouse squabbling among faculty in quest of more students, (7) a growing apathy among study populations, (8) shifting job markets and career patterns, making faculty development and retooling mandatory, (9) eroding confidence among faculty with administrators' inability to effect change, (10) insufficient confidence in the educational process by consumers, and (11) emergence of an involvement in collective bargaining options* (Crase 1980, p. 118).

Ladd (1979) found that dissatisfactions producing stress among faculty are not strictly related to those factors Crase would later identify. He contends instead that the target of instructors' criticism is teaching itself. "Most academics think of themselves as 'teachers' and 'professionals,' not as 'scholars,' 'scientists,' or 'intellectuals'—and they perform accordingly" (p. 3). Complaints about the quality of teaching come from both teaching- and research-oriented institutions. "There appears to be ambivalence about academe's principal function: teaching" (Brookes and German 1983, p. 3). Students admitted to college are grossly underprepared in basic skills, yet faculty are pressured to do research in spite of the importance of effective teaching. Faculty find themselves trapped at institutions where they must demonstrate accomplishments in research or lose a teaching job when they know that what they actually should be doing is teaching and not demonstrating proficiency in research (Ladd 1979). In a study of 213 faculty at a large, comprehensive land-grant institution, participants were interviewed regarding their perceptions about teaching. Almost half responded that they had "feelings of burnout and frustration—of heavy teaching loads and university expectations for doing research, on the one hand, and, on the other, of not having time to spend with families" (Peters and Mayfield 1982, p. 108).

One must have heard at least once a colleague comment, "It's not worth teaching—it's just not rewarded." Extrinsic rewards alone—an increase in salary and promotion in rank—do not motivate professors to improve the quality of their teaching. Intrinsic rewards are the factors that motivate effective teaching (McKeachie 1979). Faculty committees, however, refuse to consider teaching accomplishments in their recommendations for promotion (Mauksch 1980). Instead, they require a vita listing many publications. In answer to the question of why certain kinds of teaching cannot be rewarded the same as certain kinds of research, Peters and Mayfield (1982) suggest that the equivalence between teaching and research with regard to the method of application, teaching level, academic disciplines, and types of institutions to carry out such innovation should be explored further. Although faculty regard teaching in a positive manner, they are aware that they must work in a stressful organizational climate characterized by a heavy workload and an undervalued reward system. "University faculty members have a high regard for teaching, but when the reward system fails to recognize that regard they experience stress" (Peters and Mayfield 1982, p. 109).

In a study of the relationships between college finances and faculty members' assessments, involvement in college planning and governance was deemed a major factor in causing low morale among 5,000 faculty members at 93 colleges and universities (Magarrell 1982). The proportion of faculty involved in their institution's planning and governance declined from 64 percent in 1970 to 44 percent in 1980. Leadership appears to be an important factor. Administrators at private institutions involve more faculty in planning and decision making. Faculty at 10 community colleges as a group felt a loss of control, resulting in a dramatic decline in institutional spirit and concern for their institution's system of governance (Magarrell 1982).

Stress may be associated with leadership power structures. Although not enough evidence exists to establish a consistent association between democratic leadership and higher productivity, "in most situations . . . democratic leadership is associated with higher morale" (Rosenbaum and Rosenbaum 1971, p. 348). Although "high morale should not be in lieu of high productivity," it does "suggest a positive work environment, which lends itself to increased productivity" (Mitchell 1980, p. 8).

Supporting the general trend toward increasing faculty members' productivity and creativity are the findings of a study investigating the sources of stress of 1,957 faculty and administrators at 17 two- and four-year colleges (Meléndez and de Guzmán 1983). Almost one-fifth of the respondents (19 percent) reported they experienced severe stress, 43 percent indicated they experienced moderate stress, 27 percent reported mild stress, and 11 percent never felt any work stress at all. Specific job situations were found to be most stressful. For purposes of analysis, the numerous factors that generate stress among academics were distributed among three categories: those related to colleagues, those related to students, and those related to administration. In this investigation, the three sources of stress of most concern were faculty apathy, student apathy, and workload rather than salaries, job security, or diversity of students (see Figures 1, 2, and 3). Among factors related to colleagues, faculty apathy was the greatest producer of frustration, followed by team work and respect of colleagues (Figure 1). Among factors related to students, the three greatest factors were students' apathy (the lack of motivation among students), students' expectations for high grades despite instructors' belief they are not warranted, and the decline in students' entry-level ability for college-level work, in that order (Figure 2). Of the factors related to the institution's administration, workload, budget constraints, and the lack of faculty members' participation or influence in decision making, in that order, caused the greatest stress. Promotions and salaries followed closely (Figure 3).

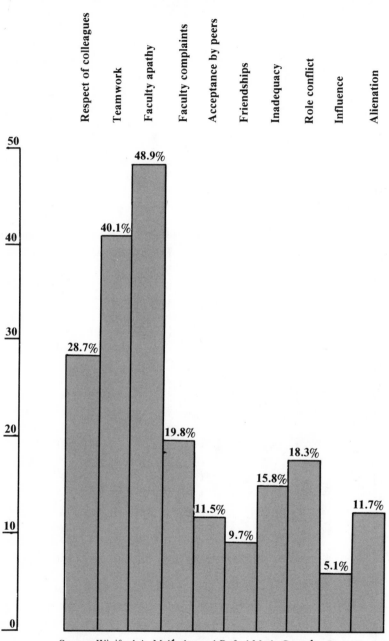

FIGURE 1
SOURCES OF STRESS RELATED TO COLLEAGUES

Source: Winifred A. Meléndez and Rafael M. de Guzmán, *Burnout: A Study of Stress in Academe* (San Juan: Inter American University, 1983), appendix.

FIGURE 2
SOURCES OF STRESS RELATED TO STUDENTS

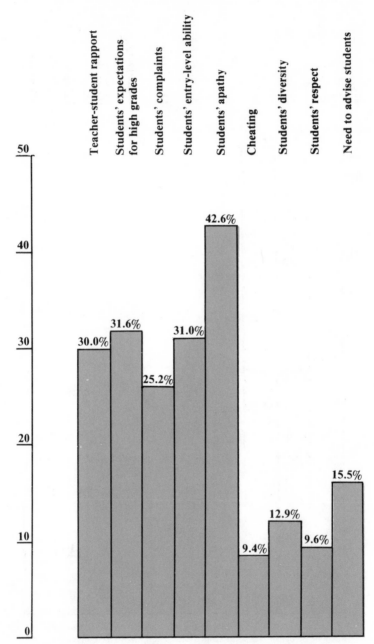

Source: Winifred A. Meléndez and Rafael M. de Guzmán, *Burnout: A Study of Stress in Academe* (San Juan: Inter American University, 1983), appendix.

Although faculty indicated workload as the third greatest source of stress among all the sources listed, the average number of teaching hours coupled with other academic responsibilities did not indicate a heavy workload. "Workload," however, includes the additional time spent preparing for "quality" teaching. Apathy, diversity, and entry-level ability of students, in addition to individual coaching and tutoring, certainly require much more preparation time from professors and make workload appear unduly heavy.

The number one source of stress was faculty apathy; almost half the respondents (48.9 percent) indicated it was a factor. Hence, in terms of their own perceptions, respondents indicated that little time is available to devote to group interaction because teaching and research consume so much time.

The individuals experiencing severe stress may reach their limits of tolerance in two to eight years if their conditions do not change. With age comes greater vulnerability to a very severe case of burnout and marked depression. As one becomes older, one has fewer reserves, and ". . .every biologic activity leaves some irreversible 'chemical scars,' " which will never be completely restored (Selye 1974, p. 28). As resources weaken, the individual's level of tolerance lessens. Thus, the person becomes more vulnerable to burnout.

Prescribing Remedies
The literature on work-related stress suggests that the *causes* of stress can be found within the person and within the work environment and that the *effects* of stress can be found in the person and in the organization (see, for example, Beehr and Newman 1978). Controlling stress therefore requires major changes in the person or the environment (Newman and Beehr 1979). Although many personal and organizational strategies for handling work stress exist, industrial therapists have not evaluated their effectiveness.

Personal prescriptions
One can deduce from Selye's philosophy of modifying *distress* to *eustress* and establishing harmony between life and the laws of Nature the code of behavior that lessens

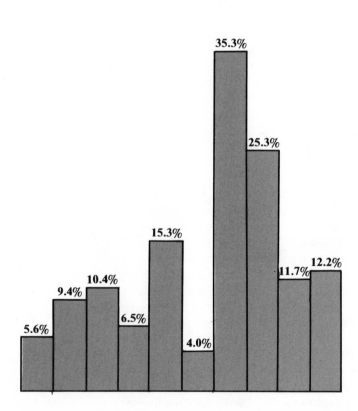

Large classes

Course assignments

Committee assignments

Role as student advisor

Evaluation process

Restrictions on academic freedom

Budget constraints

Decision-making process

Job security

Professional respect

5.6%

9.4%

10.4%

6.5%

15.3%

4.0%

35.3%

25.3%

11.7%

12.2%

FIGURE 3
SOURCES OF STRESS RELATED TO ADMINISTRATION

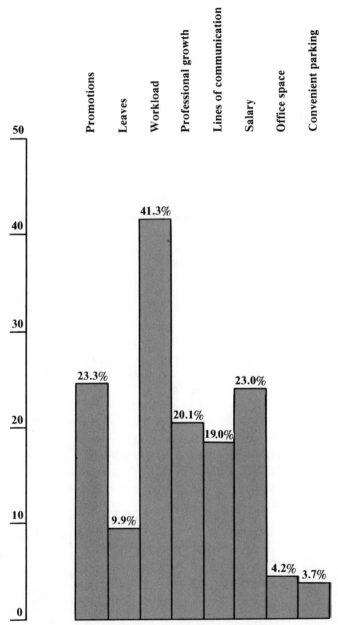

Source: Winifred A. Meléndez and Rafael M. de Guzmán, *Burnout: A Study of Stress in Academe* (San Juan: Inter American University, 1983), appendix.

stress.[1] Current laboratory and clinical work on stress emphasizes "the scientifically verifiable laws of Nature that govern the body's reactions in maintaining homeostasis and living in satisfying equilibrium with its surroundings" (Selye 1980, p. 339). Selye establishes a set of guidelines, which he calls the "philosophy of altruistic egoism" (1980, p. 341)—in other words, "be good to yourself."

1. *Find your own natural stress level and run toward what you accept as your own goal* (p. 340). In self-analysis, one considers hereditary predispositions, traditions, and expectations. With these points in mind, one can discover his level of tolerance for stress and then plan accordingly.
2. *Practice altruistic egoism* (p. 341). Use the body's energy for one's own benefit as well as mankind's.
3. *Earn thy neighbor's love* (p. 341). Learn to trust people and to feel secure by creating a support system that eventually averts loneliness.

We must learn to live by a code of ethics that accepts, as morally correct, egoism and working to hoard personal capital. The "philosophy of altruistic egoism" advocates the creation of feelings of accomplishment and security through the inspiration in others of love, goodwill, and gratitude for what we have done or are likely to do in the future (Selye 1980, p. 340).

Selye contends that a code of behavior will be developed further as a result of studying the field of endocrinology and the nervous processes. In the meantime, however, the scientific principles already discovered should serve the purpose of developing a philosophy for one's life code of ethics.

One should learn to live in a manner that does not disturb one's body. Set goals in life, pursue them, and comply

[1]Selye's concept was converted into the code of ethics for the International Institute of Stress, which is devoted to the furtherance of research on stress and to the dissemination of past and current knowledge. The institute has a stress library and documentation service containing over 150,000 entries, which are available to the general public. An international network of affiliated stress institutes and stress teaching centers is being organized (Selye 1980, p. 338).

with your expectations. Develop a positive self-image (Kozoll 1982; Miller 1979). "In other words, having a sense of
goodwill for others plus respect for oneself seems to open
such a free action for living that one seems to transcend
the petty and sometimes bitter constrictions that pop up in
day-to-day situations."*

For those who feel "stuck" in their jobs, a possible way
of dealing with the situation is by initiating change and
growth. Howard and Downey (1980) propose that the individual first make a firm decision to modify his or her life
and then develop a plan of action based on his goals. Once
the rationale is clear and the work plan has been drawn,
the next step is to act.

The individual then can use several tactics to relieve the
situation—networking, outside enrichment activities,
study, job hunting, and becoming a mentor. Networking includes an exchange of ideas and information with different
groups of people who can become acquainted with one's
work and thus serve to increase its visibility. Outside enrichment activities provide challenging tasks beyond the
daily routine of teaching. Directing a project, for example,
whether it is for research, a proposal, or a book, provides
the individual with a sense of control. Study, another alternative, does not necessarily mean taking an academic
course. It can mean taking a course like computerization
for personal enrichment or a refresher course in one's field.
Job hunting can be beneficial if one is able to regard job in-
terviews as ways of expanding professional networks and
can avoid becoming frustrated if he is not hired. Becoming
a mentor can be a fulfilling role. Besides gaining satisfaction, the other individual may someday return the favor.
"Think of creative coping as a life style," insist Howard
and Downey. "The only real barriers to self-renewal are
the limits of one's imagination" (1980, p. 144).

Several buffers can be effective against burnout and tedium.

1. Keep a log of daily pressures and joys and evaluate
   the intensity of each for one week to one month for
   the purpose of identifying and mastering patterns in
   stresses.

*Lotta Rieskohl 1983, personal communication.

> *The individual
> [who is feeling
> "stuck"] . . .
> can use
> several tactics
> to relieve the
> situation—
> networking,
> outside
> enrichment
> activities,
> study. . . .*

2. Before reappraising long-term and short-term goals, be realistic and clarify priorities.
3. Be realistic in projecting time.
4. Be aware of your personal, mental, and physical supply of energy to avoid crises.
5. Keep a balance between work and life outside your job to avoid recreating traumatic experience with persons closest to you.
6. Be aware of work stresses and recognize danger signs of burnout by acknowledging vulnerabilities.
7. Keep your sense of humor (Pines, Aronson, and Kafry 1981, pp. 143-67).

Veninga and Spradley (1981) have developed personal strategies to build immunity and prevent a recurrence of job burnout. In this process, the most important approach is understanding the nature and power of stress and how the human body responds to stress, thus allowing one to diagnose his or her own situation. The second strategy is to be aware of one's daily work stresses. Third, one should listen to the body for warning signals of chronic tiredness or depression. To prevent more stress or possible burnout in a situation one cannot change or escape, one should accept it realistically, lowering expectations for achievement by setting attainable goals during each work day. If his job is unchallenging, an individual can relieve stress by concentrating on something else. The person can substitute one form of stress for another to give the body a chance to restore energy. The individual can prevent the pressure of stress by (1) shifting from work to something else, (2) cutting back on overtime or excessive hours, (3) exercising daily, (4) pampering oneself, (5) getting involved in outside activities, (6) setting the tone for each work day, (7) rearranging one's tasks and schedule to his or her advantage, and (8) practicing favorite relaxation exercises daily (pp. 96–116).

An individual can examine the "coping process" to confront pressures in the work environment (Cooper 1981). In response to the four-stage model of stress presented by Lazarus (1967), Cooper suggests the following steps to relieve stress. The person first identifies a combination of pressures that results in physical and mental symptoms of stress and defensive behavior. This period of "shock," during which the individual builds up energy to face the future, is followed by a period of "protective withdrawal," which is categorized as "adaptive" or "maladaptive." Adaptive behavior seeks and implements solutions that eliminate the problem and prepare the individual for similar future situations. Maladaptive behavior, on the other hand, may eliminate the stressful situation but leave the individual with a feeling of anxiety and without the help needed to cope with the same situation in the future. Maladaptive behavior can become adaptive behavior, but it is important that the dynamics of the stress/coping process are concerned with how the switch is achieved, who is involved, and what actions are taken. A person suffers stress in silence either because he or she is unaware of the exact nature of the work stress or fears that colleagues or superiors will accuse him or her of the inability to cope. In assessing work pressures, an individual should diagnose the main stressors in the work environment—for academe they would include workload, clarifying one's role, minimizing role ambiguity and role conflict, improving personal relationships at work, and planning long-term career prospects—with the aid of a questionnaire or other similar means and then examine the potential work stressors that he can manage himself.

A potential victim of burnout has numerous resources available (Tubesing and Tubesing 1982). This approach to preventing or treating burnout is based on a set of assumptions within the scope of the definition of burnout.

1. "Chronic distress is a causal factor in burnout" with roots set in the workplace and/or home (p. 156).
2. "Burnout is a real personal problem," which the individual perceives as a very painful affliction (p. 156).
3. "Burnout is a human condition" occurring only to people, not to organizations (p. 156).
4. "Burnout is an energy crisis" in which the individual perceives a temporary loss of personal vitality (p. 156).
5. "Burnout affects the whole person," including intellectual, mental, emotional, social, and physical performances (p. 157).

Only the individual who is suffering can truly diagnose and alleviate symptoms of burnout. No miracle drug has been found to cure symptoms of burnout. Only the afflicted individual can remedy the pains of burnout by identifying the sources of stress, evaluating their strengths and weaknesses, and thus regaining and maintaining his vitality through a personal plan of action. To remedy burnout, however, one needs certain skills: personal management skills, relationship skills, outlook- or attitude-change skills, and stamina skills.

- *Personal management skills* can aid an individual to achieve maximum efficiency and energy by:
  1. knowing how to choose between alternatives
  2. setting goals and making steady progress
  3. committing oneself to purposeful goals
  4. spending time effectively
  5. predicting the amount of work one can handle during a specific time span.
- *Relationship skills* help control tension in the environment by:
  1. making positive contact with other people
  2. listening to develop and maintain relationships
  3. developing assertiveness to express preferences respectfully and persistently
  4. developing authoritativeness to demonstrate firmness
  5. opening a path for flight to feel quick relief from stress
  6. building one's nest to beautify surroundings for creative living or work.
- *Outlook- or attitude-change skills* help during depression by:
  1. relabeling the problem to mean something else
  2. accommodating oneself to limitations
  3. having faith to accept the mystical aspects of life
  4. analyzing the problem through self-dialogue
  5. developing imagination to release tension through creativeness and laughter.
- *Stamina skills* improve one's physical health by:
  1. exercising regularly
  2. learning proper nutrition
  3. taking care of oneself
  4. taking time to relax regularly (Tubesing and Tubesing 1982, pp. 162–66).

For individuals who have reached the last stages of burnout, professional counseling may be necessary (Freudenberger 1982). Such individuals, it is important to note, are not psychotic, having a nervous breakdown, or mentally ill (p. 177), but counseling could help the individual develop energy "to recapture a sense of self, increase confidence" (p. 184), and be able to take charge of his or her life again.

Among the many steps Freudenberger proposes is "investing more capital in the training of employees and teaching measures to prevent and lessen burnout among all kinds of helping professionals" (p. 185). Professional schools should be interested in preventing burnout and therefore should train students to remain productive throughout their careers. A survey of five types of professional schools, however—nursing, medicine, social work, business, and education—indicates misgivings from faculty "that efforts at intervention may be counterproductive" (Wilder and Plutchik 1982, p. 128). Schools seem reluctant to provide students with the knowledge needed to handle work stress in complex organizations.

Organizational prescriptions

Organizations should also be involved in the treatment of individuals suffering from burnout. Because burnout typically occurs "whenever a person with inadequate stress-management and need-gratifying skills must work in a stressful and need-frustrating work environment" (Carroll and White 1982, p. 42), "burnout is not only a very costly phenomenon for the individual, but it is also very costly for organizations" (Pines 1982, p. 189). It is unfortunate that postsecondary institutions are not aware of the high price of burnout in terms of faculty members' enthusiasm, motivation, leadership, and service to the academic community. At first glance, it would seem that administrators do not have to be concerned about faculty turnover because plenty of Ph.D.s without jobs are willing to respond with gratitude and loyalty. But the issue is one not only of turnovers; it is also a matter of productivity. "Productivity increases when one is emotionally fulfilled. . . . We must more fully understand the human factor in the managing process" (Freudenberger 1981, p. 12). An institution must be given a soul to cherish the humaneness that generates creativity and productivity. Burnout will be manifested not only in absenteeism, tardiness, and turnovers but also in general dissatisfaction and its consequence, low productivity.

Even if the economy remains relatively stable throughout the eighties, academics will continue to feel professional uncertainties that do not allow them to be as creative and enthusiastic as they wish. Institutional vitality and the "integration of individual and institutional energy, commitment, and creativity" (Maher 1982, p. 10) are important factors in faculty members' job satisfaction.

These conditions were present during the sixties, a decade that brought about a sense of generativity and vigor to higher education. Since then numerous constraints, provoked by the new economic trends at institutions, have decreased faculty members' morale and increased burnout. Unless institutions find ways of becoming more people-oriented, academia can fall into a state of psychic consumption. Should it survive, there may be scars to mend. It is therefore imperative that decision makers look further into the need for institutional vitality.

Institutional vitality involves:

- *a clearly designed and accepted mission for the unit in question;*
- *direction, attainable goals, and programs which enable fulfillment of the mission;*
- *a climate which empowers individuals to be participants in the fulfillment of the mission and to have the sense of being involved in creative, productive, and energizing work life* (Ebben and Maher 1979, p. 2).

The quality of institutional life is included in the definition of vitality:

- *to provide its members with the proper level of security and respect;*
- *to introduce, on a continuous basis, a complementary level of challenge and stimulation to call forth creativity; and*
- *to recognize those who have made significant contributions in its behalf.*

In essence, then, the quest for vitality might be said to focus on the capacity of a college or university to create and sustain the organizational strategies that support the continuing investment of energy by faculty and staff both in their own careers and in the realization of the institution's mission (Maher 1982, p. 7).

This prescription holds true for all individuals who are creative and productive, and it suggests that a faculty member should be given recognition for publishing, producing curriculum reports, trying new methods of teaching, preparing proposals, and initiating and developing exciting ideas. Labeling faculty as "productive" or "nonproductive" on the basis of the number of research articles published lessens the commendation for other creative and creditable tasks. "The discrepancy between [productive and nonproductive people] increases over time as the productive people maintain their high level and the less productive become less so" (Blackburn 1979, p. 25).

There are several truths about academic careers that decision makers should keep under their hats when planning to take advantage of faculty members' productivity and creativity.

1. Faculty productivity is predictable, depending on the age of the individual when he started becoming productive for the institution and when he received his advanced degree.
2. Faculty productivity is determined to a high degree by the institution.
3. Faculty productivity is influenced by organizational factors like leadership, support, control of the environment, and selection of colleagues.
4. Faculty productivity is influenced by time structure, which affects performance.
5. Faculty tasks and interests vary during the academic career.
6. Age is not a predictor of faculty members' productivity because the level of productivity remains more or less stable during the academic career.
7. Having a mentor and the existence of a network are important factors during the first years of an academic career.

8. Faculty productivity is stifled by uncertainty and risk taking, but competition produces better results than complacency.
9. Faculty are productive principally because of intrinsic rewards (Blackburn 1979, pp. 25–26).

From those observations it is only a short step to the following inferences about productivity and creativity:

- Faculty members' productivity and creativity have not reached their potential measures.
- Teaching would improve if faculty members' productivity increased.
- Faculty productivity and creativity could be increased by administrators' developing better working environments, working in a collective environment, and getting the assistance needed from the institution.
- Faculty need administrators who can support and challenge them and who have faith in them so that they can contribute to the institution's goals, including good teaching.
- Increasing faculty members' productivity and creativity simultaneously contributes to research in adult and career development (Blackburn 1979, p. 26).

Institutions should examine their policies on career management, making it a supportive and encouraging goal for faculty. Institutions can advocate and support research in several areas:

- faculty career patterns and institutional variations in career options
- career development for minorities and women
- the differences between faculty career development at traditional and nontraditional institutions
- the different disciplines and professions in higher education and career patterns in each domain (Mathis 1979, p. 23).

Research on career development and management, with special emphasis on the adult and the institution, is a way of giving academia the capacity to care for individuals meaningfully. A greater understanding of the human factors of productivity and creativity can once again inject some vitality into institutions of higher education. That vitality is a cure that will banish burnout.

An abundance of clinical and epidemiological investigations indicates that stressful life events are causally implicated in a number of undesirable effects on functioning and health (Dohrenwend and Dohrenwend 1974, 1980)—effects ranging from failing a test (Zausner, Farris, and Zausner 1983) to sudden death (Engel 1971). Stress has been implicated in diseases of the cardiovascular, gastrointestinal, and central nervous systems (Buckley 1983). That hypertension contributes significantly to the risk of cardiovascular morbidity and mortality is well accepted by the medical profession.

> *Hypertension has been identified as the major contributing factor in the development of cerebral vascular accidents, and it also appears to be a major factor in the genesis of congestive heart failure, coronary thrombosis, atherosclerosis, and kidney failure; thus it appears that stress per se is a factor to be considered when investigating the etiology and treatment of cardiovascular diseases* (Buckley 1983, p. 372).

But burnout need not result in only ashes. On the whole, the prognosis for recovery from burnout is good (Freudenberger 1982, p. 184).

> *Professionals can change even if they are burned out. Given the correct remediation interventions, they can return to their job and again become productive. Salvage, in this instance, may be cheaper than the alternative of dismissal and training of a replacement* (Freudenberger 1982, p. 174).

Individuals after complete exhaustion *can* recover their resistance and adaptability to almost what it was before, but they cannot be totally regained and scars will remain.

> *Complete restoration is probably impossible, since every biologic activity leaves some irreversible "chemical scars." If this is the case, we must distinguish between* superficial *and* deep *adaptation energy. Superficial adaptation energy is immediately available upon demand . . . deep adaptation energy stored away safely as a reserve. . . . The stage of exhaustion, after a tempo-*

*rary demand upon the body, is reversible, but the
complete exhaustion of all stores of deep adaptation
energy is not; as these reserves are depleted, senility and
finally death ensue* (Selye 1974, p. 29).

The individual exhibiting Type A behavior is more prone
to burnout and most probably will take longer to recuper-
ate. This situation can occur when the individual's competitive and aggressive drive activates through specific
environmental stimuli (Rosenman and Friedman 1983). The
chronic struggler's response to environmental stressors
threatens the individual's sense of control over his environment. The successful modification of Type A behavior
"depends upon intrinsic emotional components, environmental stressors, and the individual's interpretation
modification" and "muscular relaxation and techniques for
general stress reduction" (Rosenman and Friedman 1983,
p. 82).

*On the whole,
the prognosis
for recovery
from burnout
is good.*

Like Samson, whose great strength derived from his
hair, humans have great strength that derives from the laws
governing the nature of people. And like Samson, people
have to struggle and work for some goal they consider
fulfilling. It is through continuous effort, perhaps becoming
egoistic and aggressive at times, that one is able to keep
homeostatic equilibrium with the rest of mankind and with
the environment. Humans have a "natural urge to work
egoistically for things that can be stored to strengthen
[their] homeostasis in unpredictable situations" (Selye
1980, p. 340). While the commandment to "love thy
neighbor as thyself" sounds good, it is not compatible with
man's biological laws, because no creature in nature is
created solely to protect others. People must accept "as
morally correct, egoism and working to hoard personal
capital" (Selye 1980, p. 340).

As the mideighties arrive, faculty are observed experiencing greater stress and frustration in their quest for self
and personal fulfillment. They appear to have lost the
energy, vitality, and motivation to want to affect academic
matters. "Why attempt changes?" "My opinion never
counts." "They won't listen." Faculty feel powerless.
They have lost confidence in administrators. They feel
committees are a waste of time. Institutions look out only
for themselves. Therefore, they feel, they must pursue

other interests, such as research and writing. They are vastly interested in good teaching, but who in the institution cares? Decision makers will not give credit for quality teaching.

Faculty members' confidence and motivation must be restored. Additional efforts are necessary to get faculty away from adaptation to adversity, where they seem to be existing in a negative condition. It is in this state of the syndrome that they remain as stable, servile functionaries committed to the task of educating a nation without the power to be effective. The individual must be changed to promote a renewed spirit. "His activities must earn lasting results; the fruits of his work must be cumulative" (Selye 1980, p. 340).

Administrators burn out too. Even though many can resist burnout, others are prone to the syndrome. In academe, some administrators feel as powerless as faculty. They also suffer from low self-esteem. Powerless administrators tend to reward mediocrity and avoid the innovators and risk takers simply because their own skills and abilities are being undermined. They capitalize, therefore, on the only secure weapon or force they have—rules. As a result the environment is demoralized, for administrators have become sole owners of the territory in a pretentious officialdom.

But the story of burnout does not have to end with the candle burning at both ends. The story has another side— one of significant changes, where confidence, trust, and loyalty are the eternal lights that generate cohesiveness, cooperation, initiative, enrichment, creativity, and productivity. Who said that academia has burned out?

BIBLIOGRAPHY

The ERIC Clearinghouse on Higher Education abstracts and indexes the current literature on higher education for the National Institute of Education's monthly bibliographic journal *Resources in Education.* Most of these publications are available through the ERIC Document Reproduction Service (EDRS). For publications cited in this bibliography that are available from EDRS, ordering number and price are included. Readers who wish to order a publication should write to the ERIC Document Reproduction Service, P.O. Box 190, Arlington, Virginia 22210. When ordering, please specify the document number. Documents are available as noted in microfiche (MF) and paper copy (PC). Since prices are subject to change it is advisable to check the latest issue of *Resources in Education* for current cost based on the number of pages in the publication.

Abram, Morris B. 1970. "Reflections on the University in the New Revolution." *Daedalus* 99(1-2):122–40.

Adams, Edward F.; Laker, Dennis R.; and Hulin, Charles L. 1977. "An Investigation of the Influence of Job Level and Functional Specialty on Job Attitudes and Perceptions." *Journal of Applied Psychology* 62(3):335–43.

Allen, Douglas R.; Hitt, Michael A.; and Greer, Charles R. 1952. "Occupational Stress and Perceived Organizational Effectiveness in Formal Groups: An Examination of Stress Level and Stress Type." *Personnel Psychology* 35:359–69.

Anderson, C.R. 1976. "Coping Behaviors as Intervening Mechanisms in the Inverted-U Stress-Performance Relationship." *Journal of Applied Psychology* 61:30–34.

Anderson, P.W., and Larson, T.A. 1975a. *Institutional Variables Related to High Faculty Attrition.* Washington, D.C.: Association of American Medical Colleges. ED 115 169. 25 pp. MF-$1.17; PC-$5.49.

——— . 1975b. *Mobility Characteristics of U.S. Medical School Faculty.* Washington, D.C.: Association of American Medical Colleges. ED 115 168. 104 pp. MF-$1.17; PC-$11.12.

Arana, José, ed. 1977. *Trabajo y Estres.* Madrid: Editorial Karpos.

Arthur, Ransom J., and Grenderson, E.K. 1965. "Promotion and Mental Illness in the Navy." *Journal of Occupational Medicine* 7:452–56.

Ashby, W.R. 1954. *Design for a Brain.* London: Chapman and Hill.

——— . 1966. *An Introduction to Cybernetics.* New York: John Wiley & Sons.

Babbie, Earl R. 1973. *Survey Research Methods.* Belmont, Cal.: Wadsworth Publishing Co.

Baldwin, Roger. 1979. "Adult and Career Development: What Are the Implications for Faculty?" In *Faculty Career Development.* Current Issues in Higher Education No. 2. Washington, D.C.: American Association for Higher Education. ED 193 998. 44 pp. MF-$1.17; PC not available EDRS.

Ballief, Conrad A. 14 January 1980. "Giving Till It Hurts." *Chronicle of Higher Education* 19(17):64.

Bardo, Pamela. December 1979. "The Pain of Teacher Burnout: A Case History." Phi Delta Kappan 61(4):252–54.

Beck, Aaron T. 1979. "What to Do When You're under Stress." Mimeographed. Río Piedras, Puerto Rico: University of Puerto Rico.

Beehr, Terry. 1976. "Perceived Situational Moderators of the Relationship between Subjective Role Ambiguity and Role Strain." *Journal of Applied Psychology* 61(1):35–40.

Beehr, Terry A., and Newman, John E. 1978. "Job Stress, Employees' Health, and Organizational Effectiveness: A Facet Analysis, Model, and Literature Review." *Personnel Psychology* 31:665–99.

Behnke, John A.; Finch, Caleb E.; and Moment, Gairdner B., eds. 1978. *The Biology of Aging.* New York: Plenum Press.

Bender, Robert C., and Blackwell, Martha W. 1982. *Professional Expectations, Stress, and University Faculty: An Analysis.* Houston, Tex.: Southern Association for Counselor Education and Supervision.

Benson, Herbert. July-August 1974. "Your Innate Asset for Combating Stress." *Harvard Business Review* 52:49–60.

Bertrand, Ursula S. 1981. "Personal and Organizational Correlates of Role Stress and Job Satisfaction in Female Managers." Ph.D. dissertation, University of Wisconsin.

Bess, James L. 1973. "Patterns of Satisfaction of Organizational Prerequisites and Personal Needs in University Academic Departments." *Sociology of Education* 46(1):99–114.

———. 1982. *University Organization.* New York: Human Sciences Press.

Biddle, Bruce J. 1979. *Role Theory: Expectations, Identities, and Behaviors.* New York: Academic Press.

Bidwell, Charles E. 1974. "New Research on the Academic Professions." *Sociology of Education* 41(1):1.

Billingsley, Andrew. 1978. "Higher Education as a Source of Personal and Social Integration." Paper presented at the 33rd National Conference on Higher Education of the American Association for Higher Education, Chicago, March 20.

Blackburn, Robert T. 1979. "Academic Careers: Patterns and Possibilities." In *Faculty Career Development*. Current Issues in Higher Education No. 2. Washington, D.C.: American Association for Higher Education. ED 193 998. 44 pp. MF-$1.17; PC not available EDRS.

Blai, Boris, Jr. 1977. *The Views and Values of Harcum Faculty.* Bryn Mawr, Pa.: Harcum Junior College. ED 146 980. 24 pp. MF-$1.17; PC-$5.49.

Bornheimer, Deane G.; Burns, Gerald P.; and Dunke, Glenn S. 1973. *The Faculty in Higher Education.* Danville, Ill.: Interstate Printers and Publishers.

Botwinick, Jack. 1973. *Aging and Behavior.* New York: Springer Publishing Co.

Boyd, Jerry Lynn. 1981. "A Comparative Study of Holland's Theory of Person Environment Congruence and Staff Burnout Syndrome as They Relate to Job Satisfaction Tenure in Rural Community Mental Health Centers." Ph.D. dissertation, University of Illinois.

Bramhall, M., and Ezell, S. Winter 1981. "How Burned Out Are You?" *Public Welfare:* 23–27.

Brawer, Florence B. 1976. *Satisfaction and Humanities Instructors in Two-Year Colleges.* Los Angeles: UCLA. ED 128 048. 46 pp. MF-$1.17; PC-$5.49.

Bridgwater, Carol Austin. February 1983. "Women's Puny Promotions." *Psychology Today* 17(2):16.

Brod, Jan. 1971. "The Influence of Higher Nervous Processes Induced by Psychosocial Environments on the Development of Essential Hypertension." In *Society, Stress, and Disease,* edited by L. Levi. The Psychosocial Environment and Psychosomatic Diseases, vol. 1. London: Oxford University Press.

———. 1983. "Stress and Arterial Hypertension." In *Selye's Guide to Stress Research,* vol. 2, edited by Hans Selye. New York: Scientific and Academic Publications.

Brookes, Michael C.T. 1980. "Generativity, Stuckness, and Insulation: Community College Faculty in Massachusetts." Ph.D. dissertation, University of Massachusetts.

Brookes, Michael C.T., and German, Katherine L. 1983. *Meeting the Challenges: Developing Faculty Careers.* ASHE-ERIC/ Higher Education Research Report No. 3. Washington, D.C.: Association for the Study of Higher Education. ED 232 516. 54 pp. MF-$1.17; PC-$7.26.

Buckley, Joseph. 1983. "Present Status of Stress Research Related to the Development of Cardiovascular Diseases." In *Selye's Guide to Stress Research,* vol. 2, edited by Hans Selye. New York: Scientific and Academic Publications.

Bullock, William, Jr. 1968. "Control and Satisfaction in Schools of Education: An Analysis of Faculty Perceptions." ED 148 782. 28 pp. MF-$1.17; PC-$5.49.

Burke, R.J. 1976. "Occupational Stresses and Job Satisfaction." *Journal of Social Psychology* 100:235–44.

Campbell, D.B. 1974. "A Program to Reduce Coronary Heart Disease Risk by Altering Job Stresses." Ph.D. dissertation, University of Michigan.

Cannon, W. 1932. *The Wisdom of the Body.* New York: Norton.

Caplan, R.D. 1972. "Organizational Stress and Individual Strain: A Social-psychological Study of Risk Factors in Coronary Heart Disease among Administrators, Engineers, and Scientists." Ph.D. dissertation, University of Michigan.

Caplan, R.D.; Robinson, E.A.R.; French, J.R.P., Jr.; Caldwell, J.R.; and Shinn, M. 1976. *Adhering to Medical Regimens: Pilot Experiments in Patient Education and Social Support.* Ann Arbor, Mich.: Institute of Social Research.

Carroll, Jerome F.X., and White, William L. 1982. "Theory Building: Integrating Individual and Environmental Factors within an Ecological Framework." In *Job Stress and Burnout: Research, Theory, and Intervention Perspectives,* edited by Whiton S. Paine. Beverly Hills, Cal.: Sage Publications.

Cathcart, L.M. 1977. "A Four-Year Study of Executive Health Risk." *Journal of Occupational Medicine* 19(5):354–57.

Caws, Peter J. 1970. "Design for a University." *Daedalus* 99(1-2):84–107.

Chait, Richard P., and Gueths, James. May-June 1981. "A Framework for Faculty Development." *Change* 13(4):30–33.

Cherniss, Cary. 1980. *Staff Burnout: Job Stress in the Human Services.* Beverly Hills, Cal.: Sage Publications.

Chickering, Arthur W. 1980. "Adult Development: A Workable Vision for Higher Education." In *Integrating Adult Development Theory with Higher Education Practice.* Current Issues in Higher Education No. 5. Washington, D.C.: American Association for Higher Education. ED 194 008. 32 pp. MF-$1.17; PC not available EDRS.

Chickering, Arthur W., and Associates. 1981. *The Modern American College.* San Francisco: Jossey-Bass.

Cichon, Donald J., and Koff, Robert H. March 1980. "Stress and Teaching." *NASSP Bulletin* 64:91–103.

Clagett, Craig A. 1980. *Teacher Stress at a Community College: Professional Burnout in a Bureaucratic Setting.* Largo, Md.: Prince Georges Community College, Office of Institutional Research. ED 195 310. 60 pp. MF-$1.17; PC-$7.24.

Coates, Thomas J., and Thoreson, Carl E. 1976. "Teacher Anxiety: A Review with Recommendations." *Review of Educational Research* 46(2):159–79.

Cohen, Arthur M. 1973. *Work Satisfaction among Junior College Faculty Members.* Los Angeles: UCLA. ED 081 426. 8 pp. MF-$1.17; PC-$3.74.

Colasurdo, Michael Modesto. 1981. "A Descriptive Survey of Professional Burnout amongst Public School Teachers in San Diego, California." Ph.D. dissertation, University Microfilms International.

Collins, James J., and Masley, Barbara A. 1980. "Stress/Burnout Report." *Share and Exchange* 8(4).

Constandse, W.J. 1972. "Mid-40's Man: A Neglected Personnel Problem." *Personnel Journal* 51(2):129.

Cooper, Cary L. 1981. *The Stress Check.* Englewood Cliffs, N.J.: Prentice-Hall.

Cooper, C.L., and Payne, R., eds. 1978. *Stress at Work.* New York: John Wiley & Sons.

———, eds. 1980. *Current Concerns in Occupational Stress.* New York: John Wiley & Sons.

Cooper, John F. 1977. *The Morale and Teaching Effectiveness of Junior College Teachers.* University of California. ED 134 266. 13 pp. MF-$1.17; PC-$3.74.

Corwin, Thomas M. 1978. "A Research Perspective on the Mandatory Retirement Issue." In *Changing Retirement Policies.* Current Issues in Higher Education. Washington, D.C.: American Association for Higher Education. ED 193 991. 31 pp. MF-$1.17; PC not available EDRS.

Coser, L.A. 1956. *The Functions of Social Conflict.* New York: Free Press.

Coser, L.A., and Coser, R.L. 1974. *Greedy Institutions.* New York: Free Press.

Crase, Darrell. 1980. "Antecedents of Faculty Frustration." *Physical Educator* 37(3): 118–21.

Crose, K. Patricia. 1971. *Beyond the Open Door.* San Francisco: Jossey-Bass.

———. 1982–83. "Can Higher Education Be Equal and Excellent Too?" In *Underprepared Learners,* edited by K. Patricia Cross. Current Issues in Higher Education No. 1. Washington, D.C.: American Association for Higher Education.

Cummings, Thomas G., and Cooper, Cary L. 1979. "A Cybernetic Framework for Studying Occupational Stress." *Human Relations* 32:395–418.

Cunningham, William G. May 1982. "Research-Based Strategies for Fighting Teachers' Burnout." *The Education Digest:* 20–23.

Curtin, Bernadette M., and Hecklinger, Fred J. 1981. "Job-Keeping and Revitalization." Career Life Assessment Skills Series. Alexandria, Va.: Northern Virginia Community College. ED 211 175. 45 pp. MF-$1.17; PC-$5.49.

Cytrynbaum, Solomon. 1982. "Faculty Development through the Life Course: Application of Recent Development Theory and Research." *Journal of Instructional Development* 5(3):11–22.

Daley, Michael R. September 1979. "Burnout:' Smoldering Problem in Protective Services." *Social Work* 24(5):375–79.

Darrow, Morton. 1979. "Changing Values: Implications for Major Social Institutions." In *Perspectives for Leadership.* Current Issues in Higher Education No. 1. Washington, D.C.: American Association for Higher Education. ED 193 997. 26 pp. MF-$1.17; PC not available EDRS.

Delgado, J.M.R.; Roberts, W.W.; and Miller, N.E. 1954. "Learning Motivated by Electrical Stimulation of the Brain." *American Journal of Physiology* 179: 587–93.

Dohrenwend, Barbara S., and Dohrenwend, Bruce P., eds. 1974. *Stressful Life Events: Their Nature and Effects.* New York: John Wiley & Sons.

————. 1980. "What Is a Stressful Life Event?" In *Selye's Guide to Stress,* vol. 1, edited by Hans Selye. New York: Van Nostrand Reinhold Co.

Dougherty, Thomas Warren. 1981. "Role-Based Stressors: An Investigation of Relationships to Personal and Organizational Outcomes." Ph.D. dissertation, University of Houston.

Duea, Jerry. 1981. "Presidents Rate Their Duties for Time, Importance, and Stress." *Phi Delta Kappan* 62(9):649–55.

Ebben, James, and Maher, Tom. 1979. "Capturing Institutional Vitality." Paper presented at the 19th Annual Forum of the Association for Institutional Research, San Diego, May 13–17. ED 174 092. 18 pp. MF-$1.17; PC-$3.74.

Eddy, Margot Sanders. 1981. "Faculty Response to Retrenchment." *AAHE-ERIC/Higher Education Research Currents.* Washington, D.C.: American Association for Higher Education. ED 202 446. 5 pp. MF-$1.17; PC-$3.74.

Engel, G.L. 1971. "Sudden and Rapid Death during Psychological Stress: Folklore or Folk Wisdom?" *Annals of Internal Medicine* 74:771–82.

Erikson, Erik H. 1963. *Childhood and Society.* New York: W.W. Norton & Co.

————. 1964. *Insight and Responsibility.* New York: W.W. Norton & Co.

————. 1965. *The Challenge of Youth.* New York: Doubleday & Co.

————. 1977. *Toys and Reasons.* New York: W.W. Norton & Co.

Erikson, Erik H., and Erikson, Joan. 1981. "On Generativity and Identity." *Harvard Educational Review* 51(2):249–69.

Farber, Barry A., and Miller, Julie. September 1982. "Teacher Burnout: A Psychoeducational Perspective." *Education Digest:* 23–25.

Feitler, Fred C., and Tokar, Edward B. 1981. "Teacher Stress: Sources, Symptoms, and Job Satisfaction." Paper presented at the annual meeting of the American Educational Research Association, Los Angeles, April 13–17. ED 204 857. 28 pp. MF-$1.17; PC-$5.49.

————. March 1982. "Getting a Handle on Teacher Stress: How Bad Is the Problem?" *Educational Leadership* 39(6):456–58.

Ference, T.P.; Stoner, J.A.F.; and Warren, E.K. October 1977. "Managing the Career Plateau." *Academy of Management Review:* 602–12.

Fernández, David. 1983. "Stress, Instinct, and Homeostasis." In *Selye's Guide to Stress Research,* vol. 2, edited by Hans Selye. New York: Scientific and Academic Editions.

Finch, Caleb E., and Hayflick, Leonard, eds. 1977. *Handbook of the Biology of Aging.* New York: Van Nostrand Reinhold co.

Flowers, V.S., and Hughes, C.L. July-August 1973. "Why Employees Stay." *Harvard Business Review* 51:49–60.

Fox, Mary F. 1981. "Sex, Salary, and Achievement: Reward Dualism in Academia." *Sociology of Education* 54(2):71–84.

Frankenhaeuser, Marianne. 1975. "Stress on the Sexes: How They Differ." *Science News* 107(15):238.

French, John R.P., Jr., and Caplan, R.D. 1970. "Psychosocial Factors in Coronary Heart Disease." *Industrial Medicine and Surgery* 39:383–97.

————. 1973. "Organizational Stress and Individual Strain." In *The Failure of Success,* edited by A.J. Marrow. New York: AMACOM.

French, J.R.P., Jr., and Kahn, R.L. 1962. "A Programmatic Approach to Studying the Industrial Environment and Mental Health." *Journal of Social Issues* 18(3):1–48.

French, J.R.P., Jr.; Rodgers, W.; and Cobb, S. 1974. "Adjustment as Person-Environment Fit." In *Coping and Adaptation,* edited by G.V. Coelho, D.A. Hamburg, and J.H. Adams. New York: Basic Books.

French, J.R.P., Jr.; Tupper, C.J.; and Mueller, E.S. 1965. *Work Load of University Professors.* Cooperative Research Project. Unpub. research report. No. 2171. Ann Arbor: University of Michigan. ED 003 329. 278 pp. MF-$1.17; PC-$22.39.

Freudenberger, Herbert J. 1974a. "Crisis Intervention, Individual and Group Counseling, and the Psychology of the Counseling Staff in a Free Clinic." *Journal of Social Issues* 30:77–86.

———. 1974b. "Staff Burnout." *Journal of Social Issues* 30:159–65.

———. 1980. *Burn Out: The High Cost of High Achievement.* Garden City, N.Y.: Doubleday & Co.

———. 1981. "Executive Burn-Out." Lecture delivered at the Harvard Business Club, New York, October 23.

———. 1982. "Counseling and Dynamics: Treating the End-Stage Person." In *Job Stress and Burnout: Research, Theory, and Intervention Perspectives,* edited by Whiton S. Paine. Beverly Hills, Cal.: Sage Publications.

Freudenberger, Herbert J., and North, Gail. 1982. *Situational Anxiety: How to Overcome Your Everyday Anxious Moments.* Garden City, N.Y.: Doubleday & Co.

Frew, David R. 1977. *Management of Stress: Using T.M. at Work.* Chicago: Nelson-Hall.

Friedman, Meyer. 1982. "Modifying Type A Behavior Reduces Heart Attacks." *Brain Mind Bulletin* 7(16):1–2.

Friedman, Meyer, and Rosenman, R.H. 1974. *Type A Behavior and Your Heart.* New York: Alfred A. Knopf.

Friend, Kenneth. Fall 1982. "Stress and Performance: Effects of Subjective Work Load and Time Urgency." *Personnel Psychology* 35(3):623–32.

Furniss, W.T. October 1981. "Reshaping Faculty Careers." *Change* 13(7):38–57.

Gann, Maxine Laure. 1979. "The Role of Personality Factors and Job Characteristics in Burnout: A Study of Social Service Workers." Ph.D. dissertation, University of California–Berkeley.

Gardner, Ralph, Jr. October 1981. "Guard Stress." *Corrections Magazine:* 7–14.

Giammaffeo, Michael C., and Giammaffeo, Dolores M. 1980. *Executive Well-Being: Stress and Administrators.* Reston, Va.: National Association of Secondary School Principals. ED 180 134. 67 pp. MF-$1.17; PC not available EDRS.

Glazer, H.T., and Weiss, J.M. 1976. "Long-Term Interference Effect: An Alternative to 'Learned Helplessness.'" *Journal of Experimental Psychology: Animal Behavior Processes* 2:202–13.

Glazer, Penina M. 1979. "The Concept of Tenure and an Alternative." In *Tenure*. Current Issues in Higher Education No. 6. Washington, D.C.: American Association for Higher Education. ED 194 002. 21 pp. MF-$1.17; PC not available EDRS.

Goleman, Daniel. November 1979. "Positive Denial: The Case for Not Facing Reality." *Psychology Today* 13(6):44–60.

Goode, W.J. 1960. "A Theory of Role Strain." *American Sociological Review* 25:483–96.

Grahn, Joyce. 1981. *General College Job Satisfaction Survey*. Minneapolis: University of Minnesota. ED 208 716. 28 pp. MF-$1.17; PC-$5.49.

Greenberger, Robert S. 23 April 1981. "How Burnout Affects Corporate Managers and Their Performance." *The Wall Street Journal*.

Groen, J.J., and Bastiaans, J. 1975. "Psychological Stress, Interhuman Communication and Psychosomatic Disease." In *Stress and Anxiety,* vol. 1, edited by C.D. Speilberger and I.G. Sarason. New York: John Wiley & Sons.

Gross, Edward. 1968. "Universities as Organizations: A Research Approach." *American Sociological Review* 33(4):518–44.

Gupta, Nina. 1981. *The Organizational Antecedents and Consequences of Role Stress among Teachers*. Austin, Tex.: Southwest Educational Development Laboratory. ED 215 957. 97 pp. MF-$1.17; PC not available EDRS.

Gupta, Nina, and Jenkins, Douglas, Jr. 1981. *Work Role Stress among Female and Male Public School Teachers*. Austin, Tex.: Southwest Educational Development Laboratory. ED 211 497. 23 pp. MF-$1.17; PC not available EDRS.

Hackman, Richard J.; Jawer, Edward L., III; and Porter, Lyman W., eds. 1983. *Perspectives on Behavior in Organizations*. New York: McGraw-Hill.

Hall, Calvin S. 1954. *A Primer of Freudian Psychology*. New York: New American Library.

Hall, Elizabeth. June 1983. "A Conversation with Erik Erikson." *Psychology Today* 17(6):22–30.

Hartnett, Rodney T., and Centra, John A. 1974. "Faculty Views of the Academic Environment: Situational vs. Institutional Perspectives." *Sociology of Education* 47(1):159–68.

Heim, Peggy. 1980. "The Economic Decline of the Professoriate in the 1970s: What Happened to Faculty Salaries and What Are the Implications?" In *Differing Perspectives on Declining Faculty Salaries*. Current Issues in Higher Education No. 3. Washington, D.C.: American Association for Higher Education. ED 194 006. 26 pp. MF-$1.17; PC not available EDRS.

Hersey, Paul, and Blanchard, K.H. 1972. *Management of Organizational Behavior.* Englewood Cliffs, N.J.: Prentice-Hall.

Hodgkinson, Harold L. Fall 1974. "Adult Development: Implications for Faculty and Administrators." *Educational Record* 55:263–74.

House, J.S. 1972. "The Relationship of Intrinsic and Extrinsic Work Motivations to Occupational Stress and Coronary Heart Disease Risk." Ph.D. dissertation, University of Michigan.

House, J.S., and Wells, J.A. 1978. "Occupational Stress, Social Support, and Health." In *Reducing Occupational Stress: Proceedings of a Conference,* edited by A. Mclean. Publication No. 78-140. Washington, D.C.: U.S. Government Printing Office.

Howard, J.H.; Cunningham, D.A.; and Rechnitger, P.A. 1977. "Work Patterns Associated with Type A Behavior: A Managerial Population." *Human Relations* 30:825–36.

Howard, Suzanne, and Downey, Peg. 1980. "Turning Job Burnout into Self-Renewal." *Educational Horizons* 58(3):139–44.

Hulicka, Irene M. 1977. *Psychology and Sociology of Aging.* New York: Thomas Y. Crowell.

Ivancevich, J.M., and Matteson, M.T. 1980. *Stress and Work.* Glenview, Ill.: Scott, Foresman & Co.

Jacques, Elliot. 1976. *A General Theory of Bureaucracy.* New York: Halsted Press.

Janeway, T.C. 1913. "A Clinical Study of Hypertensive Cardiovascular Disease." *Archives of Internal Medicine* 12:755.

Janis, I.L. 1958. *Psychological Stress.* New York: John Wiley & Sons.

———. 1972. *Groupthink.* Boston: Houghton Mifflin Co.

Jenkins, C.D. 1976. "Recent Evidence Supporting Psychologic and Social Risk Factors for Coronary Disease." *New England Journal of Medicine* 294:987–94.

Jenkins, Craig J., and Perrow, Charles. 1977. "Insurgency of the Powerless: Farm Worker Movements." *American Sociological Review* 42(2):249–67.

Johnson, Thomas W., and Stinson, John E. 1975. "Role Ambiguity, Role Conflict, and Satisfaction: Moderating Effects of Individual Differences." *Journal of Applied Psychology* 60(3):329–33.

Jones, Mary Ann, and Emanuel, Joseph. 1981. "Preventing Burnout through Counselor Training." Paper presented at the annual meeting of the North Central Association for Counselor Education and Supervision, Milwaukee, October 16–18. ED 214 075. 12 pp. MF-$1.17; PC-$3.74.

Kafry, Ditsa, and Pines, Ayala. July 1980. "The Experience of Tedium in Life and Work." *Human Relations* 33:477–503.

Kahn, R.L. Spring 1978. "Job Burnout: Prevention and Remedies." *Public Welfare:* 61–63.

Kahn, R.L.; Wolfe, D.M.; Quinn, R.P.; and Snoek, J.D. 1981. *Organizational Stress: Studies in Role Conflict and Ambiguity.* Malabar, Fla.: Robert E. Krieger Publishing Co.

Kahn, R.L.; Wolfe, D.M.; Quinn, R.P.; Snoek, J.D.; and Rosenthal, R.A. 1964. *Organizational Stress: Studies in Role Conflict and Ambiguity.* New York: John Wiley & Sons.

Kamis, Edna. 1980. "An Epidemiological Approach to Staff Burnout." Paper presented at the 88th Annual Convention of the American Psychological Association, Montreal, Quebec, Canada, September 1–5. ED 203 253. 17 pp. MF-$1.17; PC-$3.74.

Kanter, Rosabeth Moss. 1968. "Commitment and Social Organization: A Study of Commitment Mechanisms in Utopian Communities." *American Sociological Review* 33(4):499–517.

———. 1978. "The Changing Shape of Work: Psychological Trends in America." In *Current Issues in Higher Education.* Washington, D.C.: American Association for Higher Education. ED 193 992. 19 pp. MF-$1.17; PC not available EDRS.

Kasl, Stanislao V. 1978. "Epidemiological Contributions to the Study of Work Stress." In *Stress at Work,* edited by C.L. Cooper and R. Payne. New York: John Wiley & Sons.

Katz, D., and Kahn, R.L. 1978. *The Social Psychology of Organizations.* 2d ed. New York: John Wiley & Sons.

Katz, F.E. 1968. *Autonomy and Organization: The Limits of Social Control.* New York: Random House.

Kerlinger, Fred N. 1964. *Foundations of Behavioral Research.* 2d ed. New York: Holt, Rinehart & Winston.

Kerr, Clark. 1970. "Governance and Functions." *Daedalus* 99(1-2):108–21.

Knefelkamp, L. Lee. 1980. "Faculty and Student Development in the 80's: Renewing the Community of Scholars." In *Integrating Adult Development Theory with Higher Education Practice.* Current Issues in Higher Education No. 5. Washington, D.C.: American Association for Higher Education. ED 194 008. 32 pp. MF-$1.17; PC not available EDRS.

Kneller, G. 1965. *Educational Anthropology: An Introduction.* New York: John Wiley & Sons.

Kobasa, Susanne C.; Hilker, R.J.; and Maddi, S.R. September 1979. "Who Stays Healthy under Stress?" *Journal of Occupational Medicine* 21:595–98.

Kozoll, Charles E. 1982. *Time Management for Educators.* Fastback No. 175. Bloomington, Ind.: Phi Delta Kappa Educational Foundation.

Kremer, Lya, and Hofman, John E. 1981. "Teachers' Professional Identity and Job Leaving Inclination." Paper presented at the

---

annual meeting of the American Educational Research
Association, Los Angeles, April 13–17. ED 202 851. 21 pp. MF-
$1.17; PC-$3.74.

Kyriacou, Chris, and Sutcliffe, J. 1978. "A Model of Teacher
Stress." *Educational Studies* 4(10):1–5.

———. 1979. "A Note on Teacher Stress and Locus of Control."
Journal of Occupational Psychology 52:227–28.

Ladd, Everett Carll, Jr. 1979. "The Work Experience of American
College Professors: Some Data and an Argument." In *Faculty
Career Development*. Current Issues in Higher Education No. 2.
Washington, D.C.: American Association for Higher Education.
ED 193 998. 44 pp. MF-$1.17; PC not available EDRS.

Lamson, G. 1974. *Steady State Staff Planning: The Experience of a
Mature Liberal Arts College and Its Implications*. Northfield,
Minn.: Carleton College. ED 111 297. 138 pp. MF-$1.17;
PC-$12.87.

Lazarus, Barbara, and Tolpin, Martha. 1979. "Engaging Junior
Faculty in Career Planning: Alternatives to the Exit Interview." In
Faculty Career Development. Current Issues in Higher Education
No. 2. Washington, D.C.: American Association for Higher
Education. ED 193 998. 44 pp. MF-$1.17; PC not available
EDRS.

Lazarus, Richard S. 1966. *Psychological Stress and the Coping
Process*. New York: McGraw-Hill.

———. 1967. "Cognitive and Personality Factors Underlying
Threat and Coping." In *Psychological Stress,* edited by M.H.
Appley and R. Trumbull. New York: Appleton.

Levi, L. 1971. "The Human Factor—and the Inhuman." In *Society,
Stress, and Disease,* edited by L. Levi. The Psychosocial
Environment and Psychosomatic Diseases, vol. 1. London:
Oxford University Press.

Levinson, Daniel J. 1978. *The Seasons of a Man's Life*. New York:
Ballantine Books.

Levinson, Harry. 1970. *Executive Stress*. New York: Harper &
Row.

———. May-June 1981. "When Executives Burn Out." *Harvard
Business Review:* 73–81.

Levy, R.L.; Hellmann, C.C.; Stroud, W.D.; and White, P.D. 1944.
"Transient Hypertension: Its Significance in Terms of Later
Development of Sustained Hypertension and Cardiovascular-
Renal Diseases." *Journal of the American Medical Association*
126:829.

Light, Donald W., Jr. 1974. "The Structure of the Academic
Professions." *Sociology of Education* 47(1):2–28.

Linnell, Robert H. 1979. "Age, Sex, and Ethnic Trade-Offs in Faculty Employment: You Can't Have Your Cake and Eat It Too." In *Employment Practices in Academe.* Current Issues in Higher Education No. 4. Washington, D.C.: American Association for Higher Education. ED 194 000. 21 pp. MF-$1.17; PC not available EDRS.

Long, Huey B., and Ulmer, Curtis, eds. 1972. *The Physiology of Aging: How It Affects Learning.* Englewood Cliffs, N.J.: Prentice-Hall.

Luria, Zella, and Luria, S.E. 1970. "The Role of the University: Ivory Tower, Service Station, or Frontier Post?" *Daedalus* 99(1-2): 75–83.

Lynch, James T. 1981. "Beating Burnout." Paper presented at the annual convention of the New Jersey Education Association, Atlantic City, November 12–13. ED 218 532. 16 pp. MF-$1.17; PC-$3.74.

MacBride, A. 1982. *On-the-job Stress: A Review of the Literature.* Toronto: Clarke Institute of Psychiatry.

McCormack, Patricia. 24 January 1983. "Stress Test Aims to Control Life's Strains." *The San Juan Star.*

McGaffey, Thomas N. 1978. "New Horizon in Organizational Stress Prevention Approaches." *Personnel Administrator* 23(11):26-32.

McGee, Reece. 1971. *Academic Janus.* San Francisco: Jossey-Bass.

McGrath, J.E. 1970. *Social and Psychological Factors in Stress.* New York: Holt, Rinehart & Winston.

McGregor, Douglas. 1960. *The Human Side of Enterprise.* New York: McGraw-Hill.

McGuigan, F.J.; Sime, Wesley E.; and Wallace, J. Macdonald, eds. 1980. *Stress and Tension Control.* New York: Plenum Press.

McGuire, Willard H. November-December 1979. "Teacher Burnout." *Today's Education* 68:1–4.

McKeachie, Wilbert. 1979. "Perspectives from Psychology: Financial Incentives Are Ineffective for Faculty." In *Academic Rewards in Higher Education,* edited by D.R. Lewis and W.E. Becker, Jr. New York: Ballinger.

McKenzie, Thomas Edward. 1981. "Burnout in Education." Ph.D. dissertation, University of Michigan.

Maddi, Salvatore R. 1980. "Personality as a Resource in Stress Resistance: The Hardy Type." Paper presented at the 88th Annual Convention of the American Psychological Association, Montreal, Quebec, Canada, September 1–5. Rockville, Md.: National Institute of Mental Health. ED 198 425. 20 pp. MF-$117; PC-$3.74.

Magarrell, Jack. 10 November 1982. "Decline in Faculty Morale Laid to Governance Role, Not Salary." *Chronicle of Higher Education* 25(11):1.

Maghen, Khalil; Naylor, Dawn A; and Zalut, Warren J. 1981. "Psychophysiologic Changes after Cardiac Surgery." *Psychiatric Annals* 11(7):43–47.

Maher, Thomas H. 1982. "Institutional Vitality in Higher Education." *AAHE-ERIC/Higher Education Research Currents.* Washington, D.C.: American Association for Higher Education. ED 216 668. 4 pp. MF-$1.17; PC-$3.74.

Mann, L. 1969. *Social Psychology.* New York: John Wiley & Sons.

Manuso, James S. 1979. "Executive Stress Management." *Personnel Administrator* 24(11):23–26.

Margolis, Bruce J.; Kroes, W.H.; and Quinn, R.P. 1974. "Job Stress: An Unlisted Occupational Hazard." *Journal of Occupational Medicine* 16:659–61.

Marrow, Lance. 21 September 1981. "The Burnout of Almost Everyone." *Time:* 84.

Maslach, C. 1978. "The Client Role in Staff Burnout." *Journal of Social Issues* 34(4):111–24.

———. 1982a. *Burnout: The Cost of Caring.* Englewood Cliffs, N.J.: Prentice-Hall.

———. 1982b. "Understanding Burnout: Definitional Issues in Analyzing a Complex Phenomenon." In *Job Stress and Burnout: Research, Theory, and Intervention Perspectives,* edited by Whiton S. Paine. Beverly Hills, Cal.: Sage Publications.

Maslach, C., and Jackson, S.E. 1979. "Burned-out Cops and Their Families." *Psychology Today* 12(12):59–62.

Masuda, Minorm, and Holmes, Thomas H. 1981. "Variations in Life Events in Different Groups: Clinical Significance." *Psychiatric Annals* 11(6):48–65.

Mathis, B. Claude. 1979. "Academic Careers and Adult Development: A Nexus for Research." In *Faculty Career Development.* Current Issues in Higher Education No. 2. Washington, D.C.: American Association for Higher Education. ED 193 998. 44 pp. MF-$1.17; PC not available EDRS.

Matteson, M.T., and Ivancevich, J.M. 1979. "Organizational Stressors and Heart Disease: A Research Model." *Academy of Management Review* 4:347-57.

Mauksch, Hans O. 1980. "What Are the Obstacles to Improving Quality Teaching?" In *Improving Teaching and Institutional Quality.* Current Issues in Higher Education No. 1. Washington, D.C.: American Association for Higher Education. ED 194 004. 63 pp. MF-$1.17; PC not available EDRS.

Mayer, Nancy. 1978. *The Male Mid-Life Crisis.* New York: Doubleday & Co.

Meglino, B.M. 1977. "Stress-Performance Controversy." *MSU Business Topics* 25:53–59.

Meichenbaum, D., ed. 1977. *Cognitive Behavior Modification: An Integrative Approach.* New York: Plenum Press.

Meléndez, Winifred A., and de Guzmán, Rafael M. 1983. *Burnout: A Study of Stress in Academe.* San Juan: Inter American University.

Merton, R.R. 1957. *Social Theory and Social Structure.* Rev. ed. New York: Free Press.

Meyer, John A. 1979. "Social Construction of Burnout: An Emergent Theory." Ph.D. dissertation, Boston University.

Miles, Robert H. 1977. "Role-Set Configuration as a Predictor of Role Conflict and Ambiguity in Complex Organizations." *Sociometry: A Journal of Research in Social Psychology* 40(1):21–34.

Miller, Neal E. 1951. "Learnable Drives and Rewards." In *Handbook of Experimental Psychology,* edited by S.S. Stevens. New York: John Wiley & Sons.

———. 1980. "Effects of Learning on Physical Symptoms Produced by Psychological Stress." In *Selye's Guide to Stress,* vol. 1, edited by Hans Selye. New York: Van Nostrand Reinhold Co.

Miller, William C. 1979. *Dealing with Stress: A Challenge for Educators.* Fastback No. 130. Bloomington, Ind.: Phi Delta Kappa Educational Foundation.

Miskel, Cecil, and Gerhardt, Ed. 1974. "Perceived Bureaucracy, Teacher Conflict, Central Life Interests, Voluntarism, and Job Satisfaction." *Journal of Educational Administration* 12(1):84–97.

Mitchell, Regene L. 1980. "A New Dimension: The Leader's Role in Identifying and Managing Stress in the Work Environment." Graduate seminar paper, Pepperdine University. ED 216 708. 17 pp. MF-$1.17; PC-$3.74.

Moore, Kathryn M. 1983. "Examining the Myths of Administrative Careers." *AAHE Bulletin* 35(9):3–7.

Neff, Walter S. 1977. *Work and Human Behavior.* 2d ed. New York: Aldine Publishing Co.

Neter, John; Wasserman, William; and Whitmore, G.A. 1973. *Fundamental Statistics for Business and Economics.* 4th ed. Boston: Allyn & Bacon.

Newell, Jackson L., and Spear, Karen I. 1982. "New Dimensions for Academic Careers: Rediscovering Intrinsic Satisfactions." Paper presented at the annual meeting of the Association for the Study of Higher Education, Washington, D.C., March 2.

Newman, John E., and Beehr, Terry A. 1979. "Personal and Organizational Strategies for Handling Job Stress: A Review of Research and Opinion." *Personnel Psychology* 32:1–43.

Newman, Katherine K. 1980. *Stress in Teachers' Midcareer Transitions: A Role for Teacher Education.* ED 196 868. 23 pp. MF-$1.17; PC-$3.74.

Niehouse, Oliver L. September-October 1981. "Burnout: A Real Threat to Human Resources Managers." *Personnel:* 25–32.

Oken, Donald. 1974. "Stress: Our Friend, Our Foe." *Blue Print for Health* 25(1):4–18.

Ornish, Dean. 1983. "Stress/Diet Program Strengthens Diseased Hearts." *Brain Mind Bulletin* 8(4):1–3.

O'Toole, James. 1978. "Tenure: A Conscientious Objection." *Change* 10(6):24–31.

Otto, Nelson Robert. 1980. "Professional Burnout: A Delphic Probe to Determine Its Definition, Characteristics, Causes, and Solutions." Ph.D. dissertation, University of Minnesota.

Ouchi, W.G. 1981. *Theory Z.* New York: Aron Books.

Paine, Whiton S., ed. 1982. *Job Stress and Burnout: Research, Theory, and Intervention Perspectives.* Beverly Hills, Cal.: Sage Publications.

Palmer, David D., and Patton, Carl V. 1978. "Faculty Attitudes toward Early Retirement." In *Changing Retirement Policies.* Current Issues in Higher Education. Washington, D.C.: American Association for Higher Education. ED 193 991. 31 pp. MF-$1.17; PC not available EDRS.

Pankin, R. February 1973. "Structural Factors in Academic Mobility." *Journal of Higher Education* 44:95–101.

Pardes, Herbert D. 1983. "Stress." *The Encyclopedia Americana Annual.* Danbury, Conn.: Grolier.

Parker, S., and Kleiner, R.J. 1966. *Mental Illness in the Urban Negro Community.* New York: Free Press.

Parsons, Michael M. 1977. "Against the Dying of the Light: Staff Development Confronts the 1980s. Paper presented at the National Conference on Community College Staff and Organizational Development, Zion, Illinois, October 28. ED 145 881. 10 pp. MF-$1.17; PC-$3.74.

Parsons, Talcott, and Platt, Gerald M. 1970. "Age, Social Structure, and Socialization in Higher Education." *Sociology of Education* 43(1):1–37.

Patton, Bobby. 1981. "Continued Development of Tenured Faculty." Paper presented at the 67th Annual Meeting of the Speech Commission Association, Anaheim, California, November 12–15. ED 210 753. 11 pp. MF-$1.17; PC-$3.74.

Pelletier, Kenneth R. February 1977. "Mind as Healer; Mind as Slayer." *Psychology Today* 10:35–43.

Peters, Dianne S. 1980. "Why Professors Leave: Stress in the Organization." *Professional Educator* 3(2):6–7.

Peters, Dianne S., and Mayfield, J. Robert. 1982. "Are There Any Rewards for Teaching?" *Improving College and University Teaching* 30(3):105–10.

Pettegrew, Loyd S., and Wolf, Glenda E. 1981. *Validating Measures of Teacher Stress.* Nashville: George Peabody College for Teachers. ED 213 743. 42 pp. MF-$1.17; PC-$3.74.

Pines, Ayala. 1982. "Changing Organizations: Is a Work Environment without Burnout an Impossible Goal?" In *Job Stress and Burnout: Research, Theory, and Intervention Perspectives,* edited by Whiton S. Paine. Beverly Hills, Cal.: Sage Publications.

Pines, Ayala M.; Aronson, Elliot; and Kafry, Ditsa. 1981. *Burnout: From Tedium to Personal Growth.* New York: Macmillan.

Pines, Ayala, and Kafry, Ditsa. November 1978. "Occupational Tedium in the Social Services." *Social Work* 23:499–507.

———. 1981. "Tedium in the Life and Work of Professional Women as Compared with Men." *Sex Roles* 7(10):963–77.

Pinneau, S.R., Jr. 1976. "Effects of Social Support on Psychological and Physiological Strains." Ph.D. dissertation, University of Michigan.

Quinn, R.P.; Seashore, S.; Kahn, R.; Mangione, T.; Cambell, D.; Staines, G.; and McCullough, M. 1971. *Survey of Working Conditions.* Document No. 2916-0001. Washington, D.C.: U.S. Government Printing Office.

Reed, Sally. 7 January 1979. "Teacher 'Burnout' a Growing Hazard." *The New York Times.*

Reeves, Roxanne W. 1982. *Stress in School Environments: An Administrative Perspective.* Bethesda, Md.: National Institute of General Medical Sciences. ED 214 308. 37 pp. MF-$1.17; PC-$5.49.

Reynolds, Willie, and Stecklein, John E. 1981. "A Three-Decade Comparison of College Faculty Characteristics, Satisfactions, Activities, and Attitudes." Paper presented at the 21st Annual Forum of the Association for Institutional Research, Minneapolis, May 17–20. ED 205 113. 25 pp. MF-$1.17; PC-$5.49.

Ripley, Herbert S., and Dorpat, Theodore L. 1981. "Life Change and Suicidal Behavior." *Psychiatric Annals* 11(6):32–47.

Robinson, J.P.; Athanasion, R.; and Head, K.B., eds. 1969. *Ann Arbor: Institute for Social Research.* Ann Arbor: University of Michigan.

Roeske, Nancy C. 1981. "Stress and the Physician." *Psychiatric Annals* 11(7):10–32.

Rogers, Rolf E. 1983. "Perceptions of Stress among Canadian and American Managers: A Cross Cultural Analysis." In *Selye's Guide to Stress Research,* vol. 2, edited by Hans Selye. New York: Scientific and Academic Editions.

Rosenbaum, Leonard L., and Rosenbaum, William B. 1971. "Morale and Productivity Consequences of Group Leadership Style, Stress, and Type of Task." *Journal of Applied Psychology* 55(4):343–48.

Rosenman, Ray H., and Friedman, Meyer. 1983. "Relationship of Type A Behavior Pattern to Coronary Heart Disease." In *Selye's Guide to Stress Research,* vol. 2, edited by Hans Selye. New York: Scientific and Academic Editions.

Ryan, B.F. 1969. *Social and Cultural Change.* New York: The Ronal Press Co.

Sales, Stephen. 1969a. "Differences among Individuals in Affective, Behavioral, Biochemical, and Physiological Responses to Variations in Work Load." Ph.D. dissertation, University of Michigan.

———. 1969b. "Organizational Role as a Risk Factor in Coronary Disease." *Administrative Science Quarterly* 14(3):325–36.

Sawyer, Darwin O. 1981. "Institutional Stratification and Career Mobility in Academic Markets." *Sociology of Education.* 54(2):85–97.

Schein, Edgar H. 1971. "The Individual, the Organization, and the Career: A Conceptual Scheme." *Journal of Applied Behavioral Science* 7:401–26.

Schlesinger, Sue H., ed. 1976. *The Humanities in Two-Year Colleges: Faculty Characteristics.* Los Angeles: UCLA. ED 130 721. 71 pp. MF-$1.17; PC-$7.24.

Schuler, R.S.; Aldag, R.J.; and Brief, A.P. 1977. "Role Conflict and Ambiguity: A Scale Analysis." *Organizational Behavior and Human Performance* 20:119–28.

Schwab, Richard L. 1980. "The Relationship of Role Conflict, Role Ambiguity, Teacher Background Variables, and Perceived Burnout among Teachers." Ph.D. dissertation, University of Connecticut.

Schwab, Richard L., and Iwanicki, Edward. 1981. "The Effect of Role Conflict and Role Ambiguity on Perceived Levels of Teacher Burnout." Paper presented at the annual meeting of the American Educational Research Association, Los Angeles, April. ED 202 850. 25 pp. MF-$1.17; PC-$3.74.

Schwartz, Jackie. 1982. *Letting Go of Stress.* New York: Pinnacle Books.

Schwartz, Rosalind M., ed. 1978. *New Developments in Occupational Stress.* Proceedings of a conference on occupational stress, Los Angeles, November 13. ED 201 822. 73 pp. MF-$1.17; PC-$7.24.

Schwoebel, Robert, and Bartel, Nettie R. November-December 1982. "Revitalizing the Faculty." *Change* 14(8):22–23.

Scott, Robert A. 1978a. *Lords, Squires, and Yeomen: Collegiate Middle Managers and Their Organizations.* AAHE-ERIC/Higher Education Research Report No. 7. Washington, D.C.: American Association for Higher Education. ED 165 641. 83 pp. MF-$1.17; PC-$9.37.

———. 1978b. "Uncertain Loyalists: A Brief Look at Role Conflicts among Collegiate Middle-Managers." ED 156 105. 25 pp. MF-$1.17; PC-$3.74.

———. 1979. "Robots or Reinsmen: Job Opportunities and Professional Standing for Collegiate Administrators in the 1980s." Current Issues in Higher Education No. 7. Washington, D.C.: American Association for Higher Education. ED 194 003. 28 pp. MF-$1.17; PC not available EDRS.

———. 1980. *Indicators of Institutional Vitality.* Indiana Commission for Higher Education. ED 187 242. 7 pp. MF-$1.17; PC-$3.74.

Scott, W.E., and Cummings, L.L. 1973. *Readings in Organizational Behavior and Human Performance.* Homewood, Ill.: Richard D. Irwin, Inc.

Selye, Hans. 1965. *The Stress of Life.* New York: McGraw-Hill.

———. 1974. *Stress without Distress.* New York: Lippincott & Crowell.

———, ed. 1980. *Selye's Guide to Stress,* vol. 1. New York: Van Nostrand Reinhold Co.

———, ed. 1983a. *Selye's Guide to Stress Research,* vol. 2. New York: Scientific and Academic Editions.

———, ed. 1983b. *Selye's Guide to Stress Research,* vol. 3. New York: Scientific and Academic Editions.

Sheehy, Gail. 18 February 1974. "Catch 30 and Other Predictable Crises of Growing Up Adult." *New York Magazine.*

———. 1977. *Passages: Predictable Crises of Adult Life.* New York: Bantam Books.

Shibutani, T.A. 1968. "A Cybernetic Approach to Motivation." In *Modern Systems Research for the Behavioral Scientist,* edited by W. Buckley. Chicago: Aldine.

Slater, P.E. 1963. "On Social Regression." *American Sociological Review* 39:467–78.

Snoek, J.D. 1966. "Role Strain in Diversified Role Sets." *American Journal of Sociology* 71:363–72.

The New Academic Disease

Solomon, Lewis C. 1979. "Ph.D.s in Nonacademic Careers: Are There Good Jobs?" Current Issues in Higher Education No. 7. Washington, D.C.: American Association for Higher Education. ED 194 003. 28 pp. MF-$1.17; PC not available EDRS.

Special Task Force to the Secretary of Health, Education, and Welfare. 1973. *Work in America.* Cambridge, Mass.: MIT Press.

Student, K.R. 1978. "Personnel's Newest Challenge: Helping to Cope with Greater Stress." *Personnel Administrator* 23:20–24.

Trow, Martin. 1970. "Reflections of a Transition from Mass to Universal Higher Education." *Daedalus* 99(1-2):1–42.

Tubesing, Nancy Loving, and Tubesing, Donald A. 1982. "The Treatment of Choice: Selecting Stress Skills to Suit the Individual and the Situation." In *Job Stress and Burnout: Research, Theory, and Intervention Perspectives,* edited by Whiton S. Paine. Beverly Hills, Cal.: Sage Publications.

Tung, Rosalie L. 1980. "Corporative Analysis of the Occupational Stress Profiles of Male versus Female Administrators." *Journal of Vocational Behavior* 17:344-55.

Usdin, Gene, ed. 1978. *Aging: The Process and the People.* New York: Brunner-Mazel.

Vaillant, George E. 15 December 1979. "Study Pinpoints Stress-Illness Link." *Science News* 116:406.

Van Dijkluizen, N. 1980. *From Stressors to Strains.* Lesse, Netherlands: Swets·Zeitlinger.

Van Harrison, R. 1976. "Job Demands and Worker Health: Person-Environment Misfit." Ph.D. dissertation, University of Michigan.

———. 1978. "Person-Environment Fit and Job Stress." In *Stress at Work,* edited by Cary L. Cooper and Roy Payne. New York: John Wiley & Sons.

Van Maanen, John, ed. 1977. *Organizational Careers: Some New Perspectives.* New York: John Wiley & Sons.

Vash, Carolyn L. 1980. *The Burnt-out Administrator.* New York: Springer Publishing Co.

Vaughan, George Brandt. 1982. "Burnout: Threat to Presidential Effectiveness." *Community and Junior College Journal* 52(5):10–13.

Veninga, Robert L., and Spradley, James P. 1981. *The Work Stress Connection: How to Cope with Job Burnout.* New York: Ballantine Books.

Volgyes, Ivan. November-December 1982. "Is There Life after Teaching? Reflections of a Middle-Aged Professor." *Change* 14(8):9–11.

Wallin, Franklin W. March 1983. "Universities for a Small Planet: A Time to Reconceptualize Our Role." *Change* 15(2):7–9.

Wallis, Claudia. 6 June 1983. "Stress: Seeking Cures for Modern Anxieties." *Time:* 48–54.

Wangberg, Elaine G. March 1982. "Helping Teachers Cope with Stress." *Educational Leadership* 39(6):452–54.

Wanner, Richard A.; Lewis, Lionel S.; and Gregorio, David I. 1981. "Research Productivity in Academia: A Comparative Study of the Sciences, Social Sciences, and Humanities." *Sociology of Education* 54(4):238–53.

Wardwell, W.I.; Hyman, M.M.; and Bahnson, C.B. 1964. "Stress and Coronary Disease in Three Field Studies." *Journal of Chronic Diseases* 17:73–84.

Warnath, C.F. 1979. "Counselor Burnout." *Personnel and Guidance Journal* 57:325–28.

Watkins, Beverly T. 24 March 1982. "A New Academic Disease: Faculty 'Burnout.'" *Chronicle of Higher Education* 24(4):1.

Weathersby, Rita P., and Tarule, Jill M. 1980. *Adult Development: Implications for Higher Education.* AAHE-ERIC/Higher Education Research Report No. 4. Washington, D.C.: American Association for Higher Education. ED 191 382. 67 pp. MF-$1.17; PC-$7.24.

Weaver, Peter. 1980. *Strategies for the Second Half of Life.* New York: Signet.

Westerhouse, Mary Ann. 1979. "The Effects of Tenure, Role Conflict, and Role Conflict Resolution on the Work Orientation and Burn-out of Teachers." Ph.D. dissertation, University of California–Berkeley.

White, R.W. 1963. "Ego and Reality in Psychoanalytic Theory." *Psychological Issues Monograph II.* New York: International Universities Press.

White, William L. 1980. *Managing Personal and Organizational Stress in Institutions of Higher Education.* Rockville, Md.: N.C.S., Inc.

Wilder, Jack F., and Plutchik, Robert. 1982. "Preparing the Professional: Building Prevention into Training." In *Job Stress and Burnout: Research, Theory, and Intervention Perspectives,* edited by Whiton S. Paine. Beverly Hills, Cal.: Sage Publications.

Williams, Richard H., and Wirths, Claudine G. 1965. *Lives through the Years.* New York: Atherton Press.

Wilson, Robert C.; Wood, Lynn; and Gaff, Jerry G. 1974. "Social-Psychological Accessibility and Faculty-Student Interaction beyond the Classroom." *Sociology of Education* 47(1):74–91.

Winsteed, Philip C. 1981. *The Development of Mid-Career Faculty: A Systematic Approach.* Greenville, S.C.: Pursan University. ED 205 150. 104 pp. MF-$1.17; PC-$11.12.

Wolf, S. 1971. "Reports from the Laboratory of Clinical Stress
  Research." In *Society, Stress, and Disease,* edited by L. Levi. The
  Psychological Environment and Psychosomatic Diseases, vol. 1.
  London: Oxford University Press.
Zausner, Fred; Farris, Roy; and Zausner, Roberta J. 1983. "The
  University Student: Management, Stress, and Wellness." In
  Selye's Guide to Stress Research, vol. 2, edited by Hans Selye.
  New York: Scientific and Academic Editions.

ASHE-ERIC HIGHER EDUCATION RESEARCH REPORTS

Starting in 1983, the Association for the Study of Higher Education assumed co-sponsorship of the Higher Education Research Reports with the ERIC Clearinghouse on Higher Education. For the previous 11 years, ERIC and the American Association for Higher Education prepared and published the reports.

Each report is the definitive analysis of a tough higher education problem, based on a thorough research of pertinent literature and institutional experiences. Report topics, identified by a national survey, are written by noted practitioners and scholars with prepublication manuscript reviews by experts.

Ten monographs in the ASHE-ERIC/Higher Education Research Report series are published each year, available individually or by subscription. Subscription to 10 issues is $50 regular; $35 for members of AERA, AAHE, and AIR; $30 for members of ASHE. (Add $7.50 outside U.S.)

Prices for single copies, including 4th class postage and handling, are $6.50 regular and $5.00 for members of AERA, AAHE, AIR, and ASHE. If faster first-class postage is desired for U.S. and Canadian orders, for each publication ordered add $.60; for overseas, add $4.50. For VISA and MasterCard payments, give card number, expiration date, and signature. Orders under $25 must be prepaid. Bulk discounts are available on orders of 10 or more of a single title. Order from the Publications Department, Association for the Study of Higher Education, One Dupont Circle, Suite 630, Washington, D.C. 20036, (202) 296-2597. Write for a complete list of Higher Education Research Reports and other ASHE and ERIC publications.

1981 Higher Education Research Reports

1. Minority Access to Higher Education
   Jean L. Preer

2. Institutional Advancement Strategies in Hard Times
   Michael D. Richards and Gerald Sherratt

3. Functional Literacy in the College Setting
   Richard C. Richardosn, Jr., Kathryn J. Martens, and Elizabeth C. Fisk

4. Indices of Quality in the Undergraduate Experience
   George D. Kuh

5. Marketing in Higher Education
   Stanley M. Grabowski

6. Computer Literacy in Higher Education
   Francis E. Masat

7. Financial Analysis for Academic Units
   Donald L. Walters